Teachers, Mindset, Motivation, and Mastery

Teachers, Mindset, Motivation, and Mastery

Research Translated to K–12 Practice

Amy K. Conley

ROWMAN & LITTLEFIELD
Lanham • Boulder • New York • London

Published by Rowman & Littlefield
A wholly owned subsidiary of The Rowman & Littlefield Publishing Group, Inc.
4501 Forbes Boulevard, Suite 200, Lanham, Maryland 20706
www.rowman.com

Unit A, Whitacre Mews, 26-34 Stannary Street, London SE11 4AB

Copyright © 2017 by Amy K. Conley

All rights reserved. No part of this book may be reproduced in any form or by any electronic or mechanical means, including information storage and retrieval systems, without written permission from the publisher, except by a reviewer who may quote passages in a review.

British Library Cataloguing in Publication Information Available

Library of Congress Cataloging-in-Publication Data Available

ISBN: 978-1-4758-2214-4 (cloth : alk. paper)
ISBN: 978-1-4758-2215-1 (pbk. : alk. paper)
ISBN: 978-1-4758-2216-8 (electronic)

♾™ The paper used in this publication meets the minimum requirements of American National Standard for Information Sciences—Permanence of Paper for Printed Library Materials, ANSI/NISO Z39.48-1992.

Printed in the United States of America

Contents

Foreword		vii
Preface		ix
Acknowledgments		xi
1	Bringing Growth Mindset to Reading and Writing Instruction	1
2	Rethinking Rewards and Recognition: Intrinsic vs. Extrinsic Motivation	15
3	Mastery: How to Get Comfortable with Being Uncomfortable	31
4	Autonomy and Gamification: Choose Your Own Adventure	47
5	Purpose and Relevancy: Making It Real Makes a Difference	59
6	Fostering Connection and Positivity		75
7	Metacognition: Bringing It All Together	89
Conclusion		101
Index		105
About the Author		109

Foreword

The day I met Amy Conley, I was wishing her very bad luck. See, we were both applying for the same teaching job. I had been looking for my new high school home for more than a year, and I wanted this job! I watched her walk in to her interview while I waited nervously for mine. She came out twenty-five minutes later, and I went in for mine. In shame, I admit now that I scowled at her smile as she left the office. The principal was friendly, and we seemed to connect. He seemed impressed with my experience, education, and enthusiasm. I thought I had a good chance at the job. I wondered if she had done as well.

Later that day, I learned that she had gotten the position. BUT! The principal was developing a second position—and that one went to me! I felt so lucky. But I had no idea how lucky I was.

Amy and I began teaching English together at Fortuna High a decade ago and have enjoyed working together ever since. Our first year, we evaluated "the way it had always been done." Amy and I gave each other strength to question and wonder and eventually revise the eleventh grade English curriculum together. Already by year two, we had shifted the focus from the teacher's voice to the students' skills practice.

Collaborating with Amy completely shifted the way I saw teaching. Her focus on how students are growing their skills, developing their autonomy, and shaping their future is a guiding light to me and many of our colleagues. My own teaching practice is more engaging to me and my students when I frame my instruction with growth mindset and empower them to own their learning.

The skills Amy shares in this book are crucial for those teaching leadership, shaping school culture, and coaching other activities directors and student teachers. In this helpful resource, you'll consider the answers to the following questions: *How can I teach my student leaders to rise back up when a rally flops? How do I help a student teacher walk back in front of the class when yesterday's lesson blew up in her face?* You have to build in the expectation that flops are opportunities to learn and grow. Motivation is very high when student leaders are first elected. They have a burning desire to help. But when the work outweighs the gratitude from the student body, and all they hear are the complainers, you go to work to coach their mindset. That's when we discover that the burning drive to help may have actually been extrinsic motivation—a burning drive to be *recognized*. In this book, Amy helps us realize that true leadership mastery begins in that moment. The shift of mindset redirects students and teachers onto a pathway of self-discovery and greater satisfaction in leadership development.

My work with school culture across California and with student teachers has shown me that even educators sometimes struggle with finding the intrinsic motivation to make learning the goal. This book will be with you when your students find that moment. There are ready-to-use charts, prompts, and tools that will guide your students through the metacognition required to really begin to grow. They are the scaffolding your students need as they retrain their brains to see their mistakes as opportunities, and to see their learning as truly theirs. Amy has provided researched-based reasoning behind each of her key principles, activities you can begin using in class tomorrow, and reflections for your own growth as an instructor.

Amy's focus on student mastery and mindset has only become richer and more helpful to me as she has developed her own mastery of the subject. These days, we include our students in the discussions of their own growth toward mastery. Every school year working with Amy moves me more into collaboration with my students as we help them see their own education as a journey they can lead, shape, and value, rather than a sentence to be endured.

I just want to declare here in print: I was wrong on that day when I interviewed for my job. I should not have wished her out of the job—and I'm so very grateful for the principal who saw the value in both of us. I am incredibly grateful to have joined our teaching team together and to have been supported, inspired, empowered, and befriended by this incredible educator and friend.

Even better, I'm so excited for you, dear reader! This book, and Amy's guidance, will move you forward in your teaching practice and move your students forward in their personal learning journey. May I introduce you to my inspiring, passionate, kind, and brilliant friend? You'll be so glad you met.

Raven Coit,
Fortuna High English teacher and activities director;
writer, researcher, and presenter on school culture and values

Preface

It was so frustrating as a new teacher with 150 young souls to guide every day to be given a binder of "really great curriculum," a state-approved textbook, and foolproof worksheets and not be able to predict which lessons would work, which would bomb, and which great class at the beginning of the year wouldn't meet its potential in the second semester. I experimented on the little darlings, like all good teachers do, taking note of which methods worked for me and which didn't. And I read and I questioned.

One summer day, I was reading *Drive* by Daniel Pink in a campsite in Oregon with my family, and all of the working strategies that I had picked up in teaching for a decade suddenly gelled into a cohesive whole as Pink described the tenets of Edward Deci and Richard Ryan's self-determination theory. I started the journey of reading and researching about positive psychology and experimenting on my classes with a scientifically relevant hypothesis!

In education, we discuss and study engagement (how keyed into school students seem to be). Engagement has been defined as attention plus compliance, involvement by parents, or even regular attendance. For example, expensive programs touted by educational consultants promise to increase student engagement and make them more connected to their academic lives and the school community. When the business world discusses employee or customer engagement, it means how likely they are to leave the company.

Both definitions depend, though, on the intrinsic motivation enjoyed by the student, employee, or customer. More and more psychologists and business leaders are harvesting the ideas of positive psychology and intrinsic motivation to keep and develop their employees and customers, or, as you may call them, students.

Positive psychology emerged from the idea that science had studied psychological dysfunction and abnormality for 100 years and came up with improved treatments, medications, and predicted outcomes, but had not yet studied the behaviors and internal processes of happy, effective people. Mihaly Csikszentmihalyi, Edward Deci, Richard Ryan, Martin Seligman, Barbara Fredrickson, Carol Dweck, and other psychologists began to study conditions of optimal psychological function. Their research has snowballed and showed patterns that influence video games, social media, corporate human resources, and education trends.

As an educator for the last 16 years in high school and early online college courses, I've been urged to increase engagement without pundits, the media, or administrators necessarily knowing that engagement is an effect of an internal process in students, intrinsic motivation, or that scientific research uncovers new ways to increase intrinsic motivation every year.

As educators, we want classrooms and curriculum to get kids interested, hook at-risk students in the education community, increase their self-acceptance, and lead to college and career success. Effective classrooms scaffold students' skills from where they start to make all of that possible, but a prescriptive curriculum, teacher scripts, killer worksheets, or a 10-to-1 student–teacher ratio does not necessarily change the control our students feel over their own minds. How we discuss and frame classroom work has the largest influence on what students get out of the writing and worksheets and mandatory minutes of instruction.

When we talk about engagement in education, that's what we mean, that students are connected and invested in their learning in a way that transcends different classroom structures, rally days, substitute teachers, and holiday breaks. In short, we want to foster intrinsic motivation in our students.

In this book, I tried to take the best of positive psychology from the last 30 years and distill it to usable techniques and classroom talk for the literacy classroom, so that education focuses on the important thing: developing learners from the inside out.

Acknowledgments

I'm so lucky to always have the support of my parents Sally and Milton Conley, Byron Barker, my children Geneva and Philo, and my large and loving family.

My readers, Holly Calcote, John Dinger, Gini Wozny, Jackie Waggoner, Byron Barker, Raven Coit, Geneva Rose, Melanie Luster, Heidi Gundlach, Jessica Pierce Gillespie, Jared Ourique, Elyse Dorman, Doris Gonzalez, Connie Osbourne, and Rachel Watson, worked to make my writing more clear and helpful. All writing faults belong solely to me.

Chapter One

Bringing Growth Mindset to Reading and Writing Instruction

The most powerful tool educators have to motivate student learning is not a curriculum. It can't be bought, and it doesn't come with binders, checklists, or worksheets. How we frame learning when we talk to students about their literacy and potential has the power to change their minds about their minds. Growth mindset changes how students connect to their learning and potential by helping them choose learning over labels.

Carol Dweck's *Mindset* has led to experimentation in classrooms and classroom procedures. It isn't necessary to change the curriculum substantially; teachers can change the framing of learning, the feedback given, and how it is delivered—coaching children to be their best selves. Students want and need the power to take back their education and goals. The foundational research of positive psychology, the study of human behaviors that cause positive emotion and increased life satisfaction, explains much of what works in education and what doesn't, but teachers without knowing the research are feeling their ways, using trial and error with the methods suggested in teacher education programs without knowing *why* certain techniques work.

Teachers need not change their curriculum as much as their basic assumptions about learning and growth. Without changing a single reading, teachers can transform their classrooms by changing their mindset and the mindsets of their students.

CAROL DWECK'S RESEARCH

We teach because we believe that our students can grow their minds, grow their perspectives, and grow their futures. Since 1983, Carol Dweck of

Stanford University has been quietly studying how children's theories of their own intelligence influence their output. Her 2006 book *Mindset: The New Psychology of Success* explored the growth and fixed mindsets she found in her studies of children and adults.

Dweck's early, simple experiment in her research was to give middle school students two different lines of feedback after they'd completed a math test. Some students were told they did well on the test and must be good at math. Another set of students were told that their hard work and perseverance had helped them do well on the test. That's it.

Then the researchers followed those students for a while. Students told they were good at math didn't have an increase in life success as might be expected. Actually, they were less likely to want to take another math test soon and less likely to want to try difficult math problems. Students praised for their *effort* had different results. They agreed to additional math tests and expressed excitement at difficult problems.

More research, student interviews, and following students through years of school led Dweck to realize students who believed in fixed intelligence—possibly because an adult had told them they were intelligent or good at math or an amazing artist—also seemed to believe that those labels could be lost, that their intelligence was innate. Either they had enough intelligence or they didn't. They believed different tests and challenges could "find them out." Over time, fixed intelligence resulted in taking fewer academic chances, general unhappiness, stress in school, and lower life success in studies that followed those same students over fifteen years.

In her experiment, Dweck and her colleague Lisa Blackwell also discovered that some kids, in a sense, loved to fail. These children *wanted* the difficult math puzzles that they couldn't easily solve, whereas the children with a fixed mindset avoided these problems because they feared failure. Dweck didn't know what to think about these students, the ones who cheerfully expressed that a problem was kicking their butt and that they couldn't wait to try it again or bring it home to try it another way.

Eventually, Dweck's longitudinal research led her to two important conclusions: (1) expressing traditional ideas about intelligence to children (in regard to grades, standardized tests, high-stakes essay tests, tracking of students, IQ testing, etc.) eventually created learners who lacked belief in their ability to grow their minds, and (2) emphasizing growth, revision, goal setting, and using failure as a tool led to happier and more motivated learners.

Learners that use growth mindset are more academically successful, report more life happiness, and respond to adversity better over the course of their lives. That's exactly what we want for our students, and how we talk to them about learning influences which mindset they use. It's a lesson worth teaching and reinforcing.

STANCE: GROWTH MINDSET FOR THE ADULTS

For some teachers, the hardest part of instilling growth mindset in their students will be learning it and modeling it themselves. Some teachers were labeled smart from elementary school through college and chose teaching to follow the pattern of being the smart person in the room, the one who gets it. Most teachers didn't fail in school, and some see education as a place where if you do what's assigned and follow the rubric, you never have to fail.

Even if they've learned growth mindset in other parts of their life—hello, relationships and financial planning!—they may be pretty attached to being the smartest person in the room.

A teacher, let's call her Ms. Jacobs, says that she's the only intellectual in her classroom. She believes it's her job to get her students to think with the same academic rigor she does by reading the classics and that she doesn't have time to teach *how to learn* (goal setting, metacognition, etc.). If she shares her writing at all, it's to show a published piece that they can aspire to achieve with their own intellectual development.

Clearly, teaching growth mindset will be more problematic for Ms. Jacobs than for other teachers because she doesn't model growth mindset herself. She labels disengaged students as lazy, unmotivated. But she also hasn't shown them how or why work is learning. As Henry L. Roediger and Mark McDaniel argue in *Make It Stick*, when learning is easy, it doesn't last long-term or apply across different situations. When the learning process is hard or uncomfortable, it actually sticks longer and can be used in more settings. The same is true in learning writing techniques.

Application Story

I didn't start out actively looking to model failure for my students. As a new teacher, I wanted to look authoritative because only eight years separated me from the high school seniors I taught. Eventually, I discovered that to get my students to think like writers, I had to model real writing: the mess, the brainstorming, and the revision. And I had a revelation: They learned more about learning when I modeled it!

Adulthood doesn't come with a mystic ability to know the answers without asking questions or how to write without working at it. Asking questions, being open to failure as part of the process, and exposing the work of writing modeled for my class how to do the very things that could make them successful college students and adults.

GROWING READING

Most educators are always working on becoming better readers and writers. You probably are, too—whether you read novels, short stories, essays, poetry, recipes, comic books, Lego instructions, maps, and Facebook statuses or work toward better scientific and mathematical reading skills. Many writers work toward reading as a writer. Despite high school students commenting that they have been reading since second grade and don't need practice or new skills, good readers know that we're all still growing.

Strange as it may sound, try to stop telling your students that they're good readers. They work hard at reading, they persevere, they have many reading strategies when texts become more difficult, but telling kids they are good readers has the same fixed labeling problem as telling students they are good at math. If they just "are" good readers—innate and unearned—they can lose that label by not understanding reading from a new field.

This can be seen in second grade classrooms when children shift grudgingly from picture books to chapter books, worried about giving up the title of fastest reader or most books read, worried that if reading isn't easy, they aren't good at it. This can be seen in fifth grade with students who would rather reread a favorite (again!) than struggle with the next level of a novel with point-of-view shifts, more difficult vocabulary, and more complex syntax.

In twelfth grade, this appears as the student who tells their teacher they've been a good reader since third grade, and they "just don't like to read" and "never take notes" because "it's right up here," they say, gesturing at their heads. The fixed idea of being a "good reader" keeps students from growing their skills to meet more challenging cognitive demands.

WRITING IS HARD WORK

Exercise the writing muscle every day, even if it is only a letter, notes, a title list, a character sketch, a journal entry. Writers are like dancers, like athletes. Without that exercise, the muscles seize up.

—*Jane Yolen*

No one is born a writer, despite what our students think. A child may dream of someday becoming a writer, but imagine that happening magically, automatically, like a degree conferred. They don't imagine the practice, the daily drills, the carving out of time, and the revision. They think that when they are a "good" writer, first drafts about anything they want to write will be enthusiastically published.

When students argue that they're not good writers, they participate in that same magical thinking. They haven't read as writers, practiced daily, learned different genres, revised, or asked for feedback, but their writing is not as good as Stephanie Meyers/Suzanne Collins/J.K. Rowling/Kristin Cashore or any of their writing beacons. If, as writing educators, we believe that all students can learn to write well, we have to dispel the myth of the "good writer."

Growth mindset helps. Like Jane Yolen, we can label writing as exercise with students. At the beginning of the year, teachers can position themselves as literacy coaches, and students will work on writing *flexibility*, *strength*, *endurance*, *speed*, and *technique*. Like athletes, we're going to mix up drills to improve performance from different angles, putting it all together for the big game (or placement test or term paper or short story competition). They can keep a writing portfolio to track their growth and conference about their growth periodically.

Through physical education and sports, many students understand that fitness requires practice. Like Michael Jordan said, "I've always believed that if you put in the work, the results will come." That analogy can give them a growth mindset for their writing as well.

Flexibility

Flexibility in the classroom means being able to write in different genres for different audiences and purposes. Yes, students can write an academic essay, but how about a poem, an essay for web publication, or a cover letter? They can write informally to persuade others (see Facebook, emails, text messages, etc.), but can they write formally for a general audience to inform on the same topic?

Flexibility Exercise for Students

1. Choose a topic, like birds
   - Now write a story
   - Write a persuasive paragraph
   - Write a poem
   - Write a prompt explaining ones you can see in your neighborhood
2. Rewrite a paragraph to persuade a five-year-old
3. Rewrite your piece into a two-minute elevator speech
4. Read-around for reading flexibility: instructions, a page from a novel, football, plays, poetry, and a math textbook page. What different strategies do you use?

Strength

They hate and then love the *strength* exercises that begin the year. Strength means that it's the most efficient, clear, and detailed writing they can produce with their skills. We learn to write précis: short analytical paragraphs of five sentences or less that contain a source's main idea, organization and persuasive techniques used to support that idea with evidence, audience and value assumptions, and purpose for reader. It's a lot of information in a little bitty space. We practice and revise until they can write a précis for an article or a painting or a textbook in five minutes, controlling their register and passive voice for maximum strength.

Strength Exercise for Students

1. *Pull out a paragraph you've already written*
   - *Revise for passive voice*
   - *Revise to add a complex and compound sentence*
   - *Add rhetorical questions*
   - *Add parallelism*
   - *Add sensory details*
   - *Add adjectives*
   - *Add evidence*
2. *Read a dense, new text using at least three strategies talking through your thinking. Reread.*

Endurance

We begin classes often with *endurance* writes. Endurance builds throughout the year, training their hands and minds to compose for longer and longer time periods. "Write nonstop for four minutes about your relationships with animals." Nonstop because research by Virginia Berninger and others suggests that the motion of writing turns on the composition parts of our brain. In order to write longer, more complex work, writers need to increase how long their hands and minds can persevere.

Endurance Exercise for Students

- *Two-minute write, describing your day*
- *Four-minute write, listing your goals for the year*
- *Six-minute write, explaining your relationships with animals*
- *Six-minute write, rhyming a poem about winter*

Speed

Speed drills begin a few months through the year, after students have worked on strength and endurance. Maintaining focus, and moving body and mind faster, is a key element in developing speed and fluency. The best writing requires revision, but until we have something on the paper, there's nothing to revise. Sometimes quick and dirty composition is the way to make progress on a difficult prompt. Remind students that at this stage, ideas count more than neatness. This will free them up to get something on paper that they can later revise. Time limits will also force them to push forward when they are extending past their comfort zones.

Speed Exercise for Students

- Write a page describing your house in four minutes
- Draft a summary of today's reading in five minutes
- Read/skim a page of reading for two minutes

Technique

Most of grammar instruction gets relabeled as *technique* in the classroom: being able to use a colon before a long list, splice together sentences with a semi-colon, qualify for time or place with an introductory clause, and so forth. The more techniques students learn, the more control they'll have over their writing. Just like a tennis player will be more successful if they know how to hit with their forehand and backhand and volley shot, writers can write harder and better with more skills.

Technique Exercise for Students

1. *Practice your writing techniques by:*
   - *Writing a sentence with a colon*
   - *Writing a sentence with semi-colon*
   - *Using a list of adjectives*
   - *Using an introductory clause*
   - *Using an alliteration*
   - *Using touch, or tactile, imagery*

GROWTH MINDSET AND COMMON CORE

Dweck's work was included in the 2013 Department of Education report "Promoting Grit, Tenacity, and Perseverance: Critical Factors for Success in the 21st Century," and seven California districts agreed in 2014 to assess students using growth mindset as part of a two-year pilot program that could someday replace standardized testing.

The new Common Core literacy standards ask teachers to do just that, have students write in different and mixed genres, for different purposes, and to different audiences. Good writing mixes exposition, storytelling, and persuasion.

GROWTH MINDSET AND WRITING FEEDBACK

You put so much thought into this essay. It really makes me understand Shakespeare in a new way.

—Carol Dweck, *Mindset* (p. 178)

Feedback matters. Like Dweck's original study, the feedback given to writers shapes how they perceive their current skills, and more importantly, how they perceive their ability to improve and grow. Rubrics that give old-fashioned feedback like "10/10. You're a great writer and don't need to fix anything!"

Table 1.1. Growing Growth Mindset with Feedback

Right now you say …	Instead, you could say …	Why
Good job!	I can really see your effort in revision.	Praising effort and process encourages writers to keep trying (Dweck).
You're a good writer.	Those drafts paid off in sentence variety and imagery.	Encouraging growth instead of fixed mindset makes for happier people in charge of their progress (Dweck).
You don't know how to use semi-colons.	You haven't mastered semi-colons YET.	The power of YET suggests growth and mastery (Dweck and Pink).
Please revise.	Improved topic sentences and transitions between paragraphs would improve your paper's structure and readability.	Specific reader-focused feedback might seem nitpicky, but helps writers feel purpose of revision.
This is great!	This introduction has all of the needed components and reads clearly. A stronger attention-grabber would better hook your reader into this strong argument.	This seems like a lot of feedback, but fostering growth mindset in students means having students realize that even effective writing could always be revised for improvement. Pieces aren't finished; they're at a resting point.
0/0	Shoot! You misread the task. Reread the prompt and discuss with me. You can redo this writing to practice this skill whenever you're ready.	If it's worth a student learning a skill, they still need to learn the skill even if they failed the first time. They may even have deeper and longer-lasting learning by struggling with the idea first.

can hurt kids more than the criticism we used to worry would hurt their self-esteem.

REFRAME FAILURE

We're all afraid to fail sometimes. Even when we know that failure is a chance at growth, a chance to try again, there can be an ache in the gut at attempting something we really want that's outside of our comfort zone. But being afraid to fail can translate into being afraid to try, or maybe even worse, trying a skill without believing you can do it eventually.

Our expectations for success influence our effort. Research from Heather Barry Kappes and others argues that the cliché of positive thinking, while inspiring, doesn't make for better performance. Visualizing success is reward enough in itself that causes people to not push themselves to succeed. Thinking about what could go wrong *and doing it anyway* is the way we build skills and competence. That means that teachers and students will sometimes fail. Failure needs to be safer in the classroom.

Think about your classroom: What happens when a student attempts a reading or writing assignment and isn't successful? Is there a chance to revise? Or a chance to reflect and try it again with different strategies? According to the research into learning by Roediger, McDaniel and others, a chance to relearn and reapply skills increases the likelihood of remembering the material and applying the skills across content areas. Translation: We all need to fail more.

Attempting something difficult and learning from the experience is the epitome of growth mindset. We should aim to pair students, and ourselves, with tasks that are challenging enough to make us uncomfortable, but within our eventual mastery zone. This can be new and uncomfortable thinking for us and our students. Practice and patience at getting used to that unease is the first step. Attempting the difficult should be encouraged in our classrooms and not punished with poor grades.

THE POWER OF YET

"Yet" is our most powerful tool for giving constructive feedback. "Students haven't mastered capitalization rules *yet*." This three-letter word indicates that growth is expected, that learning is in progress. We are all a work in progress. Students can handle our criticism when it is paired with our belief in them and their ability to learn.

At one time in education, people believed that students needed us to build their self-esteem. Research by Ryan T. Howell, David Chenot, Graham Hill, and Colleen Howell and the last twenty years of education in the United States have instead shown that competence builds confidence. Being able to overcome perceived obstacles and continuing to grow skills and knowledge makes people believe they can succeed. That is the reason Carol Dweck found in the longitudinal studies that adults who exhibited growth mindsets in more parts of their lives reported more general life happiness.

TEACHERS AND WRITERS TALK ABOUT GROWTH MINDSET

I don't know that I am a good writer. However, I didn't struggle much with writing as a K–12 student. I suppose I grew those skills through reading. When I was a kid I thought I might grow up to be a novelist so I took a real interest in writing.

As for instilling a growth mindset, I think that's probably a matter of encouraging reflection within students. If they can become more aware of their writing practice, then they have an opportunity to consider how they might change that practice, even experimentally.

Digital media does a lot to change process and feedback. To start, it's easier to have a larger audience for your work, so that's more feedback. It opens a range of possibilities for process from having multiple authors on a single piece (e.g. Wikipedia) to employing a range of media.

—*Alex Reid*

About Alex: Alex Reid is an associate professor and director of composition and teaching fellow at the University of Buffalo. He is the author of *The Two Virtuals: New Media and Composition*, the co-editor of *Design Discourse: Composing and Revising Professional Writing Programs*, and the blogger of Digital Digs: An Archeology of the Future.

Take-away: Reid, a digital media-writing instructor, argues that writing and learning online is more of a growth process simply due to the give-and-take relationship between writer and reader. Revision, insertion of new information, and the forming of argument in conjunction with readers means that online publishing allows for a new kind of growth mindset.

Writing is alive and can change and be shared. It's a work in progress and not just what you turn in for a grade.

—*Melanie Downing*

About Melanie: Melanie Downing is a sixth grade teacher at Redwood Preparatory Charter School.

Take-away: Downing proposes meeting kids where they are in writing skills and pushing all of her students to surprise themselves with what they can accomplish. Class blogs are published and commented on and reedited. Students are encouraged to help each other edit and clarify. History Day, science fairs, story competitions, and class anthologies provide authentic audiences for finished products from blogs and editing. The school has Google accounts for every child, and they use both blogs and email to exchange and comment on work. Editing is ongoing, encouraging growth, because every child is a good writer if they revise enough.

> *I've probably always been better at [writing] than I am at other things (e.g., hitting a curveball, doing a physics problem set). But the way I've tried to get better is through the old tried-and-true three-part method: practice, practice, practice.*
>
> —Daniel Pink

About Daniel: Daniel Pink is best-selling author of *Drive*, *To Sell Is Human: The Surprising Truth about Moving Others*, *The Adventures of Johnny Bunko: The Last Career Guide You'll Ever Need*, and *A Whole New Mind: Why Right Brainers Will Rule the World*.

Take-away: Sharing with students the work and practice of even best-selling authors helps to dispel the "magical myth" that writing is easy. When researching this book, I emailed Daniel Pink my idea and asked questions about the topic with no belief that he would respond; it was a shot in the dark. He emailed me back during a timed essay in my sixth period class. I don't have a poker face, and my excited fidgeting and facial gestures blew the students' concentration.

When my students heard the reason, I was amazed at the teaching moment that happened. Knowing that I'm writing a book makes them work on their own writing more; they ask about my progress, and some have even offered to read and give feedback. Practice, practice, practice: changing your own mind about learning takes small steps repeated over and over.

> *You can teach even kindergarteners goal setting. Have them reflect on how they've grown. How did you do that? And their answer becomes practice, hard work, I didn't give up. Struggle is okay. Challenges are okay. Kids are in charge of their own growth, and you are in charge of helping them learn to learn.*
>
> —Lisa Jager

About Lisa: Lisa Jager is the principal of Redwood Preparatory Charter School.

Take-away: Jager has inspired a whole movement in our community. Together with a handful of other reform-minded teachers, she created an entire charter school based on research from Dweck, Love and Logic, Responsive Classroom, Habits of Mind, and Marvin Marshall. The core philosophy is that teachers should function as coaches to help students become their best selves. Students keep notebooks where they write about their learning process in different subjects. Instead of getting frustrated with not mastering something instantly, students say, "I'll try it again tomorrow this way."

How Can Teachers Model Growth Mindset?

There are many ways teachers can model a growth mindset. For example, it is acceptable for teachers to say, "I don't know," to a student's question. Of course, many of us learn the hard way in the beginning, trying to come up with an answer in order to prove our knowledge of the content, but those efforts often fall flat and sound disingenuous. In such instances, when a teacher is willing to admit that they are not the purveyor of all of the information and can model how to go about finding an answer, it contributes to a classroom environment in which everyone—teachers and students—are learning together.

This kind of experience is also authentic, meaning that the teacher remains sensitive and attuned to classroom dynamics, as well as students' needs and perspectives. Taken to an extreme, a fixed mindset implies that the teacher is all-knowing and infallible, and that mistakes are inherently bad. Quite the opposite is true. Growth cannot occur without some degree of failure. It is the reflection and the learning process that is prompted by a failure or shortcoming that allows for meaningful growth and lifelong learning to take place.

LEARN MORE

What to Read

- Adams, Jane Meredith. "Measuring a 'Growth Mindset' in a New School Accountability System." *EdSource*. May 5, 2014. Web.
    This article explains the pilot program to replace standardized testing with a system more growth mindset oriented.
- Atwell, Nancie. *In the Middle: New Understandings about Writing, Reading, and Learning*. Portsmouth, NH: Boynton/Cook, 1998.
    Atwell's book changed how middle and high school teachers thought about reading and writing instruction and introduced writers' workshop to the mainstream.

- Brown, Peter C., Henry L. Roediger, and Mark A. McDaniel. *Make It Stick: The Science of Successful Learning.* Cambridge, MA: Belknap of Harvard University Press, 2014.

    Psychologists Roediger and McDaniel study how to learn and how to remember. This book explains the research on learning and remembering for students, teachers, and parents.
- Dweck, Carol S. *Mindset: The New Psychology of Success.* New York, NY: Random House, 2006. Print.

    Dweck's book provides research and stories to show the power of growth mindset in changing academics, business, and relationships.
- Dweck, Carol S. "The Secret to Raising Smart Kids." *Scientific American.* Jan. 1, 2015. Web. Feb. 16, 2015.

    This article connects her research to the classroom and parenting. Especially helpful are the ways to phrase encouraging failure.
- Easley, Shirley-Dale, and Kay Mitchell. *Portfolios Matter: What, Where, When, Why and How to Use Them.* Markham, ON: Pembroke, 2003.

    This book is an excellent practical guide to hows and whys of using portfolios and conferencing with elementary school students. Many practical tips and handouts to use in the process.
- Flynn, Thomas, and Mary King. *Dynamics of the Writing Conference: Social and Cognitive Interaction.* Urbana, IL: National Council of Teachers of English, 1993.

    This has research into the cross-curricular evidence of higher-level thinking due to conferences. Especially relevant in light of Common Core.
- Howell, Ryan T., David Chenot, Graham Hill, and Colleen J. Howell. "Momentary Happiness: The Role of Psychological Need Satisfaction." *Journal of Happiness Studies* 12.1 (2011): 1–15. Web.

    This article connects autonomy and relatedness to momentary happiness and autonomy, competence, and relatedness to long-term happiness.
- Kappes, Heather Barry, Elizabeth J. Stephens, and Gabriele Oettingen. "Implicit Theories Moderate the Relation of Positive Future Fantasies to Academic Outcomes." *Journal of Research in Personality* 45.3 (2011): 269–78.

    This research disproves the idea of visualizing success to make it happen and instead suggests planning for worst cases helps prepare people to overcome challenges.
- Kaufman, Douglas. *Conferences & Conversations: Listening to the Literate Classroom.* Portsmouth, NH: Heinemann, 2000.

    This text addresses using portfolios and conferencing in the classroom as a method of professional and personal growth of the teacher.
- Pink, Daniel H. *Drive: The Surprising Truth about What Motivates Us.* New York, NY: Riverhead, 2009. Print.

Pink explains the business consequences of the research by Mihaly Csikszentmihalyi and others connecting intrinsic motivation to mastery, autonomy, and purpose.

What to Watch

- *The Power of Yet*. Prof. Carol Dweck. TEDx, Sep. 12, 2014. Web. Jan. 25, 2015.
    Dweck explains how communicating our expectation of their growth helps students work through being uncomfortable.
- *You Can Learn Anything*. Khan Academy, Aug. 19, 2014. Web. Jan. 25, 2015.
    Sal Khan's video explains how growth mindset means that we can all learn and become better at what we do, one small step at a time.

Chapter Two

Rethinking Rewards and Recognition
Intrinsic vs. Extrinsic Motivation

Why did you decide to work in education? Why do you work? What motivates you? No matter how it's phrased, in professional development workshops with National Writing Project or National Council of Teachers of English, educators answer:

- "That aha moment when they surprise themselves with what they can do."
- "The kids keep me young and my thinking fresh."
- "I love helping them reach their goals."
- "To model for my own children that they can have a job they love."
- "The relationships I build with students and staff."
- "I love the challenge and getting better."

They don't list the money, benefits, school vacations, or societal respect. And not just because they're teachers. Nicholas Epley tells a story in chapter 4 of his book *Mindwise* about research done at Toyota's New United Motor Manufacturing, Inc. (NUMMI) plant in Fremont, California, where they surveyed managers and assembly line workers about their motivation to work. The managers wanted to build better cars and teams, but they expected their employees to be motivated by time off, bonuses, raises, and raffle prizes. That's not what happened.

The research at NUMMI parallels the work of Mihaly Csikszentmihalyi, Edward Deci, and Richard Ryan. In opposition to everything we think we know about motivation and rewards, once people's needs are met, extrinsic rewards detract from employee performance, rather than increasing it. Extrinsic rewards can actually break employee performance.

That's what happened at the NUMMI plant. Employees who made their quota for the day of parts would be entered in raffles for prizes, big and small. Shifts that had the fewest attendance issues got small yearly bonuses. But there wasn't a system in place for employees to talk to managers about scheduling, safety concerns, or suggestions about efficiency. The managers' expectations that employees would run like hamsters on wheels for more treats had demoralized employee morale so much that it was the worst performing plant in the United States.

The plant received an overhaul to the Saturn brand and a complete change in employee motivational philosophy but kept the same employees. Away went the bonuses and prizes; instead, managers asked employees how to make the plant better. Employees asked to be cross-trained to add variety to their jobs and see how the whole system worked. They wanted a say in how and where they worked. They wanted new challenges and less micromanaging.

Working in other parts of the manufacturing resulted in suggestions to make their work more efficient and the cars safer. In three years, the plant went from the least efficient to the most efficient, a model of what intrinsic motivation can do.

Since then, Wall Street and Main Street have started rethinking employee rewards. Google, directorate of health services (DHS), and others have pioneered telecommuting, 20 percent time, flexible scheduling, employee evaluation—relying on self-determination theory to get better results than annual bonuses ever did. At Google, 20 percent time resulted in, among other innovations, Gmail, a project that developer Paul Buchheit created to manage his own email flow, as detailed in *The 20% Doctrine* by Ryan Tate.

However, teachers are intrinsically motivated, and so are their students. The implications for education have trickled down as well, with reform-minded educators and schools experimenting with giving students more control over how they take in information, project-based learning to increase purpose, and some schools, and famously the University of California, Santa Cruz, doing away with grades.

Schools must reframe and rethink the rewards systems of grades, incentives, testing bonuses, and earning school store credit for academic achievement. None of those systems are supported by the research. Instead, public

Table 2.1. Doing It for the Goods

You give ...	Instead, try ...	Because ...
Gift certificates	Junk	Rewards that have worth detract from
Collectibles	Cheap stickers	the intrinsic motivation that comes
Free books	High fives	from being recognized in front of
Money	Group claps	peers for behavior you value.
Candy	Knuckles or fist bumps	
Bookmarks	Call-and-response	
Cool stickers		

recognition of traits and hard work that people value about themselves can move learning and school culture.

FORTY YEARS OF RESEARCH ON MOTIVATION

Psychologists and researchers Edward Deci and Richard Ryan created a movement of psychology in 1990 when they began their work on self-determination theory. The theory and its subsets point to the factors of internal motivation that push people to become better versions of themselves: relatedness, autonomy, and competence. Twenty-five years later, their theory has spawned offshoots that shape research in medicine, relationships, finance, video games, and environmental sustainability, not to mention parenting and education.

Early motivation and behavior research extrapolated that, like rodents' problem-solving lever reward delivery systems or mazes, humans worked, played, and loved for what we could get materially from those actions. The research of Deci and Ryan and many others shows that extrinsic rewards provide short-term and self-limiting motivation, while humans are more complexly motivated than rats running mazes for treats.

We want to become better and to experience connection with others and to have control over our own minds and lives. That may seem obvious, but it explains the surprising truth of what motivates us and what doesn't.

Extrinsic rewards seem to make intuitive sense. We behave in a certain way to get something—prizes, grades, new cars, bonuses, and toys. We know that works because we've seen it in business, television, and of course, early on, in school.

Except that, according to forty years of behavior research headed by Edward Deci and Richard Ryan, this system of reward doesn't work. Or, at least, not as we've been told. A bonus can motivate you to work more hours but not to think more or be more productive or creative. In fact, once basic needs are met, extrinsic rewards insulate against creativity, cognitive growth, and increased emotional connection.

A simple experiment led by psychologist Teresa Amabile: Researchers approach primary students drawing pictures and ask them questions about why they drew them and how the activity makes them feel and take pictures of the art. Then the researchers tell the kids they like the art so much that they would like to pay them to take photos of future drawings. The amount offered varies in different experiments.

You would guess that the children would clamor to make money by coloring pictures they already enjoyed making. Most children agree to this deal but, while actually creating art for money, report less enjoyment creating the work. Some don't want to even finish the next piece of art. The art they make is simpler. And, most worryingly, the next time they are offered art materials, they are less likely to want to create again. You might think it's because they didn't offer the kids enough money. But the more money the researchers offer, the stronger the negative effect.

The self-determination research sparked by Edward Deci and Richard Ryan suggests that offering extrinsic rewards for activities that people are already intrinsically motivated to enjoy actually demotivates those behaviors. Extrinsic motivation can work to motivate people to do tedious tasks without purpose. That shouldn't be our education system.

Humans are intrinsically motivated to want to learn and communicate their learning, to become more capable, to create change, to create social connection. Funny thing—that's pretty much all of language arts instruction. The good news is that we already teach the good stuff that students want to learn. The bad news is that years of being extrinsically pushed to succeed in school have made students only want to do it for the payout. Good news: we can change that paradigm.

How do you discuss rewards and punishments in your classroom? When teachers are asked this, sometimes they respond that they don't have rewards and punishments in their classrooms. Hmm, why do you show movies on some afternoons when everyone has passed a test the day before? What happens to students when their behavior distracts from classroom learning? What is the ice cream for every student who improved their test score about? Certificates for honor roll and attendance?

As teachers we've created or inherited a bunch of systems that attempt to push and pull student behavior. Many work, some don't, but do we know why?

THE JAR OF MARBLES

"You earn a marble every time I see you being good. When the jar is full, your class earns a prize. If you aren't well behaved, I take marbles out."

Your childhood classrooms had marble jars, or corn kernels, or bouncy balls, or shells. So do the classrooms in most of America. It seems like a classic case of bribing kids for good behavior. It's not—at least when done well.

There are some key components to this reward system that make it work: public recognition of valued behavior, behavior inherently valuable to students and learning, and working as a team for a goal. Often times reward systems work simply because they provide public recognition to peers for behaviors they themselves value and feel good about their selves for doing.

It isn't the prize that motivates people; trophies aren't inherently valuable (check out the prices of trophies at thrift shops if you have any doubt). It's the *recognition* for effort. Everyone can see the marbles go in the jar when Miguel carries enough books for his whole table without being asked.

Which brings us to the next key aspect: the behavior needs to be inherently valuable to the students. A teacher who rewards students for doing nice favors for her, bringing her snacks, wearing her favorite color, or just cleaning her workstation, will find a jar that fills very slowly.

If those behaviors can be made about the students and what they value about themselves—they're thoughtful, they have good memories, they're tidy—there's motivation. Part of the reason marble jars work is that they give teachers an opportunity to explain about behaviors that build competency and community: helping others, creating efficient systems, learning skills, and trying hard.

The final aspect is community. Classes earn marbles together for working together for team prizes. Humans are hard-wired to be social, to work together toward goals. Students experience positive peer pressure to be their best selves, and the prize also creates community. Students don't earn individual erasers for filling the marble jar, and gift certificates for ice cream are not given to each kid. They earn pajama day for the whole class, or extra recess time together, or another group positive experience. It's not about a bonus or a trip to the school store.

Even the incentive programs touted as effective, often using token economies to school stores as an example, have limited usefulness. They can affect behaviors like attendance and turning in homework but don't seem to affect creativity and cognitive growth. Paying elementary students for test scores, like the Eric Bettinger study, "Paying to Learn: The Effect of Financial Incentives on Elementary School Test Scores," has shown surprising and problematic results. They move compliance-oriented behavior, not minds and engagement.

In the Bettinger multi-year study, student performance only improved in math, and only the first year, and all scores suffered after the incentive program ended. In the most effective incentive programs, small and public rewards for behaviors like attendance, reading time, and on-task time can work because extrinsic rewards can move behavior and, when paired with metacognition and strengths-based character work, create long-lasting feedback loops of intrinsic motivation.

For example, a small public reward can get students to spend more time reading. School culture that values and recognizes readers allows students to feel good about their extrinsically originated behavior that is then intrinsically reinforced (LeBlanc). Teachers know that we have to get kids to school before we can help them learn, but incentives for academics don't belong in the classroom. Again, as Amabile's research shows, extrinsic rewards detract from creativity, cognitive growth, and empathy.

CLASS PIZZA PARTIES AND OTHER REWARDS TO THINK ABOUT

So they filled their marble jar (or some recent graduates didn't get married, pregnant, or arrested before April), and it's time for that promised pizza party. Having relationships and experiences with students is important; breaking bread (covered with sauce and cheese!) creates community.

As previously discussed, the research is pretty clear they should be rewarded for behavior, not academic achievement, but some teachers have another worry. A total of 15.8 million children in 2013 suffer from food insecurity, according to the U.S. Department of Food and Agriculture. Using food as a reward for those students is detrimental to learning and behavior. Remember when basic needs aren't met yet, rewards can actually negatively distract from the desired emotional connection and cognitive growth. For students who are hungry, the promise of food distracts from the intended learning and behavior modification.

As Rose Sita Francia, co-principal of Hoopa Valley Elementary School with 92 percent socioeconomically disadvantaged students, explains:

> We want to be careful to not disvalue that some of our students are hungry. For them, food is an important reward and linking it to reading has consequences. If the teacher feels the need to have a snack program, and it's important and should be provided by the school in those communities, it needs to be separate—not a reward. It can be as simple as thinking about timing. I sometimes see teachers say, "When you're reading, I'll give you a snack." Great idea, but rewarding kids for reading makes it less intrinsically rewarding. Snack and reading are natural partners, they'll build up good feelings about reading and feeling safe, but the snack shouldn't be dependent on reading. It should be more like, "I want a reward of picking my own books, and I know I'm going to get the snack anyways." Additionally students can start snacks and then dig into their book boxes. The reading is the reward then. Reimbursable meals, free and reduced nutrition break, partnering with parent groups, and grants: there are many ways to get snacks into schools without making them rewards. Kids should have food available if they're hungry with no strings.

Meals and treats have a place in the classroom, but using them as rewards for academic behavior can backfire and leave poor students hungry and resentful unless managed with thought for timing and impact. Similarly, food as a reward for after testing misses the fact that some students need food before testing in order to be able to concentrate.

> **Toothpaste Samples, Cheap Stickers, and Random Re-gifts**
>
> I have prize quizzes all the time in my classroom, but I don't reward. Useless prizes with no worth move my students to work harder and participate more. Key components of a prize system focused on learning are public recognition for behavior and knowledge valuable to them and their learning goals that aren't worth much more than bragging rights. Some students will be motivated by teacher recognition, some peer recognition, and some peer competition, so make sure that your system has all three characteristics. Teenagers are surprisingly motivated by cheap stickers, because they use them as evidence of academic success and bragging rights. Younger students might be too distracted by even stickers and need high fives or stamps instead.

DO YOUR SCHOOL PUNISHMENTS REFLECT THE VALUE OF READING AND WRITING?

Was that a weird question? In some schools, students misbehaving in class earn punishments like silent reading time, extra writing assignments, or community service. There's a way to incorporate all of those activities into the school culture management. But they can't be punishments. When an activity is a punishment, adults send the message that those are behaviors to be avoided.

School-wide silent reading times during the school day at times when students tend to be unruly—like after recess or lunch—make sense, providing a quiet and independent break in the day. Allowing, not requiring, students to read or write during detention makes sense; the punishment there is the lack of choice in where they are.

Some schools offer a writing task, having to explain in writing how their behavior affected themselves and others, that asks them to reflect and change behavior, a useful metacognitive practice focused on growth. Restitution programs make sense as well—a student detracted from the learning community and, to fix the problem, needs to help the learning community by putting away books and cleaning whiteboards. The logical consequence of staying after school to finish what the student chose not to finish in class also works.

Assigning a five-hundred-word essay on a book for ten tardies denigrates the wonderful and powerful skill we have to teach. Required reading in after school detention sends the same message—no matter how much we want that time to ultimately benefit the child. Consequences in your classroom should follow the same internal logic. Students who choose not to do the required reading for the team activity will have to read first by themselves while everyone begins, so that they have the knowledge to move ahead.

Students who routinely shout out answers and talk over other students will not be assigned a book to read and book report as punishment. Assigning reading and writing as punishments negates the intrinsic motivation of those activities. Again, the words we say, the reasons we give, the ways ideas are framed, matter in the messages we give students about learning and literacy.

THE MORE STANDARDIZED TESTING AND GRADES MATTER, THE MORE THEY HURT LEARNING

High-stakes testing has an inherent problem. According to the research about learning and motivation done by Deci, Ryan, and Amabile, the more testing matters for students and teachers, the more the test becomes a controlling factor that impedes autonomy and positive feeling about the self. The stress of testing actually causes poorer test results. The more the student or school needs to test well, the more testing itself detracts from testing performance.

As teachers, we have little or no control over whether standardized testing happens in our classroom. We do have control over how we talk to students about testing. Taking the stance that "Of course we'll try our best because that's what we always do" and "Testing is an opportunity to see what we know and what we need to work on more" are ways to dial back the pressure to do well on the tests and instead focus on the test as a snapshot of current learning. Classrooms focused on growth mindset can discuss test and grades as indicators of where more work is needed without attaching shame.

That means that testing-based and grades-based rewards also cause a long-term problem trying to activate short-term results. News stories about schools offering students $20 for every standardized test where they improve their score from the year before or $100 for making honor roll are examples of

Table 2.2. Talking Back to Test Rewards

You say ...	Instead, try ...	Because ...
High scorers will be given ice cream sundaes.	Students who try hard during the test will earn time to learn a subject of their own choice.	Rewards can change effort, not academic performance (Amabile).
$20 for every score improved.	Do your best.	High extrinsic rewards detract from concentration (Ryan).
This score will determine your placement and future.	Test scores show what you should work on next.	Tests are opportunities to assess learning (Dweck).
Test well, so you can get extra recess.	Tests will show what you need to learn or review next.	Learning is the prize (Deci).

schools that have increased the stress with testing, making the students who need the reward the most distracted from the actual academic performance needed to test well.

The schools are probably just trying to ensure kids try instead of simply filling in bubbles, and rewards can move effort and especially attendance. But for every student who is already trying on tests and wants to earn an extra $20, the offered money will keep more children from reaching their academic goals.

REFOCUSING ON LEARNING AS THE PRIZE

At a formal presentation in front of hundreds of community members, the senior said, "So we have to do this project about ..." The student talked for several more minutes, but when his principal and coach asked a question after the presentation, it began, "So you *get* to do this project and ..."

The difference in wording is small, subtle, and important. Students who think that school is something they *have* to do miss the learning and growing they *get* to do. Learning is the prize. That small shift in language, for parents, teachers, and students, dramatically changes the school experience.

Phrasing testing, assignments, and writing as learning opportunities can make a small but real cultural difference in classrooms. "Have to" statements, mandatory hoops without explanation, promote external locus of control issues, where students feel their work is punishment, mostly because it's out of their control.

Changing our language helps give control over their minds back to students and makes learning a reward again, based on the research by Edward Deci and others on external locus of control in schools. Unfortunately, his research also suggests that the more students appear to need external control because of timidity or inappropriate behavior, the more those students have been controlled in the past and the more they need autonomous support.

One way to do this is through more opt-in educational activities. Students are innately excited about learning, so they push for these already in most schools. Think about how kids ask for clubs, field trips, new books in the library, other books by [blank] author, or to play astronaut or solid, liquid, gas tag during recess. The more we provide opportunities in class, the more students will choose learning above and beyond the course requirements.

Students who have completed the reading in class get to use the class time for controversial discussions based upon the text. It could be as simple as listing, like Amazon, "if you liked this reading, try this and this." A local teacher keeps copies in his classroom of his favorite novels. Students who finish assignments early can borrow a book and discuss the big ideas with him. Although the work is worth no credit and won't be tested, students find that

Table 2.3. Rethinking Praise to Avoid Controlling Language

You say …	Try saying …	Because …
You performed up to your ability.	How do you think you did?	Students can assess themselves better than teachers may expect. Their estimation of their work means more when it's self-generated (Deci).
You have a lot riding on this, but you'll do great.	What are your goals for this assignment?	Being afraid to fail keeps people from their best performance (Dweck).
These scores are important for middle school/high school/college.	I know you'll do your best.	External goals, even when attained, demotivate people (Ryan).
Good girl!	Let me know if you need help.	Females especially can find non-specific praise controlling and respond better to supportive language (Deci).
Good job! Your scores affect my performance reviews.	You used your strategies and kept at it!	Using strategies and previous competencies make people more successful than external and controlling forces, and reminding them of past success can encourage them to push for the next goal (Deci & Top 20 APA).
Great job!	Effective integration of evidence into your analysis in the body paragraphs.	Excessive praise on basic tasks transmits the idea that the teacher expects less from some students, decreasing academic confidence (Top 20 APA).

opportunity highly motivating. Sometimes students opt to stay in at recess or lunchtime to write and get feedback on their creative writing.

All of these are examples of teachers being supportive of learning that students already find intrinsically motivating; there is no reward or recognition needed. Teachers may be so trained in the philosophy of "catching them being good" that they may want to lavish praise on students when honest encouragement and supportive appreciation is more than enough to make students feel heard and understood.

TALKING ABOUT GROWTH WITH CONFERENCES AND PORTFOLIOS

As Edward Deci argues in *Why We Do What We Do*, when recognition or rewards are used with controlling language, the effect can be the opposite of what's intended. He cites Richard Ryan's study that even praise can be seen as controlling when it focuses on the speaker and their expectations. Realistically, learners need to know the expectations for assignments, but the wording of feedback can have either positive or negative impact. When praise is used as a reward, instead of as honest and supportive feedback, the learner can feel controlled, causing a loss of intrinsic motivation.

TEACHERS AND REWARDS

Perhaps ironically, teachers know much about extrinsic and intrinsic motivation by how we're treated by other adults. The intrinsic motivation of teaching—connection to students, purpose in helping kids, and ever-increasing mastery and challenge as we're asked to do more—is sometimes used as justification for low pay and stressful working conditions. The thinking goes that we should love our jobs so much that we don't need to be paid well.

The converse idea is that since teachers are low paid, their work is generally low societal value—the old "those that can't do, teach" nonsense. Difficult and fulfilling work shouldn't be used as a justification for paying teachers so little that they must worry about their families or take second jobs, both of which distract from employee effectiveness. That said, most schools have a flattened pay schedule compared to the private sector, and thus pay raises are used less as reward systems.

Unfortunately, in recent decades, the carrot and sticks of bonuses for standardized testing performance has done what rewards do, distract from the actual purpose of teaching—learning. Standardized tests can provide an accurate snapshot of student learning, but offering teachers rewards or bonuses for student scores exemplifies the problem of throwing rewards in the wrong direction.

As the research continues to show, rewards to students for coming to testing days could work, but rewarding for thinking distracts and impedes performance. Teachers need to be creative, focused, and emotionally connected to students for student academic success—all dimensions repressed by reward systems. Psychologist Edward Deci also found that the pressure teachers receive for better performance trickles down to students and creates a more controlling, and thus less motivating, educational experience for students.

Even districts often get staff reward systems wrong, choosing to feature staff members randomly, having staff compete in student test performance for gift certificates, or give rewards for years worked, practices that Wall Street firms have found make the best workers frustrated. These practices don't recognize behaviors that teachers value among themselves and instead often reward teachers for merely putting in the time.

Good teacher recognition programs, like good student recognition programs, don't need to have monetary value, do need to be public, and do need to recognize behaviors that teachers value. Suggestions might include gag gifts presented at the next staff meeting for the teacher who finished their grades first or wrote new curriculum or mentored the new teachers. Student-voted teacher of the quarter or district-chosen department teacher of the year are also meaningful ways to motivate staff and highlight the behaviors and cultures the school wants to encourage.

TEACHERS AND WRITERS TALK ABOUT REWARDS AND MOTIVATION

There's no single recipe. But for autonomy, teachers would give students more freedom to choose what they write about. On mastery, the keep is quick, specific, relevant feedback that leads to a sense of making progress. (For instance, getting a writing assignment back from the teacher three weeks after you've written it isn't all that helpful. However, seeing how your writing at the end of the year compares to your writing at the beginning of the year can be useful.) On purpose, teachers ought to make a better case for why writing is important—something with greater depth and nuance than "because it's good for you" and "because it's in the curriculum."

—Daniel Pink

About Daniel: Daniel Pink, in his best-selling book about intrinsic motivation, *Drive*, argued that workers need autonomy, purpose, and mastery to feel their jobs worthwhile. He argues that students need intrinsic motivation instead of rewards.

Take-away: Pink's *Drive* makes a compelling argument for why traditional rewards and bonus systems discourage creativity and cognitive functioning. Although Pink focuses on business models, the research also applies to children and educational systems. In this email interview with Daniel Pink, he expostulates how the research would apply to communication education.

> When teachers are the daily manifestation of educational ideals, usually enshrined within schools' mission statements, they are better able to model intrinsic motivation. If we truly value lifelong learning, compassion and tolerance, global awareness, and active citizenship, then these beliefs must be expressed in what we prioritize and what we practice. While there is a need to assess student learning, a sanctions-based system becomes geared toward extrinsic motivation, expediency, and control—and the school and classroom culture naturally follow in a similar fashion. Conversely, when the norms, policies, and structures are reflective of intrinsic motivation, the emphasis is not necessarily on outcomes for their own sake (and correspondingly, compliance and competition), but on the teaching and learning process, autonomy, support, increased efficacy, and ultimately, growth.
>
> —David Bosso

About David: Dr. David Bosso studies education and teacher motivation and also teaches social studies at Berlin High School in Connecticut. Bosso earned Connecticut 2012 Teacher of the Year and 2012 National Social Studies Teacher of the Year.

Take-away: Bosso argues convincingly that the extrinsic rewards systems used on teachers hurt students by affecting teacher mindset and distracting them from student learning, the ultimate goal of education systems.

LEARN MORE

What to Read

- Amabile, Teresa. *Growing Up Creative: Nurturing a Lifetime of Creativity*. New York, NY: Crown, 1989. Print.
    Dr. Amabile explains her psychological research into creativity and intrinsic motivation.
- Belkin, Lisa. "Does Rewarding Children Backfire?" Motherlode. *New York Times*, Nov. 14, 2008. Web. June 18, 2015.
    This parenting article explains the problems of over-rewarding kids with stuff.
- Bettinger, Eric P. "Paying to Learn: The Effect of Financial Incentives on Elementary School Test Scores." *Review of Economics and Statistics* 94.3 (2012): 686–98. Web.

This article explains a randomized, multi-year study of the effects of paying American elementary students for better test scores.
- Deci, Edward L., and Richard Flaste. *Why We Do What We Do: Understanding Self-motivation.* New York, NY: Penguin, 1996. Print.
   Deci distinguishes between rewards and recognition, and explains how controlling recognition language demotivates learners, especially women.
- Epley, Nicholas. *Mindwise: Why We Misunderstand What Others Think, Believe, Feel, and Want.* New York, NY: Vintage, 2015. Print.
   Dr. Epley's book explains how we know others less than we think and judge that others are more extrinsically motivated than we are ourselves, to everyone's detriment.
- Flanagan, Linda. "How Teachers Can Motivate Students of Any Age." *MindShift.* KQED, Oct. 22, 2014. Web. 18 June 2015.
   This article details how to increase student intrinsic motivation.
- Jones, M. Gail, Brett D. Jones, and Tracy Y. Hargrove. *The Unintended Consequences of High-stakes Testing.* Lanham, MD: Rowman & Littlefield, 2003. Print.
   This book examines, among other topics, how the rewards systems distract the schools and students who have the most to lose from high-stakes testing.
- Kohn, Alfie. *Punished by Rewards: The Trouble with Gold Stars, Incentive Plans, A's, Praise, and Other Bribes.* Boston: Houghton Mifflin, 1993. Print.
   Kohn critiques how the education system relies on extrinsic motivators, squelching kids' love of learning.
- Kohn, Alfie. "For Best Results, Forget the Bonus." *The New York Times.* Oct. 16, 1993. Web. Feb. 27, 2015.
   This classic article explains how intrinsic motivators have shifted in importance in the business world.
- Moen, Phyllis, Erin L. Kelly, and Rachelle Hill. "Does Enhancing Work-Time Control and Flexibility Reduce Turnover? A Naturally Occurring Experiment." *Social Problems.* U.S. National Library of Medicine, Feb. 1, 2011. Web. June 18, 2015.
   Researchers examined employment histories for various companies and discovered that employee autonomy over hours decreased employee turnover. Although some schools have gone to team teaching to increase flexibility, most educators are tied to school day schedules.
- Raq, Harish R. "Want to Keep (and Motivate) Your Best Employees? It's Not about the Money." *Fast Company.* Aug. 11, 2011. Web. June 18, 2015.
   This article critiques the bonus system in business as an effective motivator.

- Ryan, Richard, and Edward Deci. "Self Determination Theory." *Selfdeterminationtheory.org.* 2015. Web. June 22, 2015.

    The Self Determination website organizes the thirty years of research by topic, including basics on the theory and its implications.

- Tate, Ryan. *The 20% Doctrine: How Tinkering, Goofing Off, and Breaking the Rules at Work Drive Success in Business.* New York, NY: Harper Business, 2012. Print.

    This book explains how flexible scheduling and intrinsic motivations have powered technological innovations.

What to Watch

- "RSA Animate - Drive: The Surprising Truth about What Motivates Us." *YouTube.* Apr. 1, 2010. Web. June 18, 2015.

    Bestseller Daniel Pink details in this animated video how extrinsic rewards fail to make employees more effective.

Chapter Three

Mastery

How to Get Comfortable with Being Uncomfortable

Kids, and some adults, think that if it's easy for you, you're good at it, and if it's not easy, you should stop. There's a problem with this idea, of course. Actually, there are a few problems.

- The higher levels of any skill are not easy for anyone. No matter his talent, Piet Mondrian was not able to paint "Gray Tree" on the first try. Writers also work at it. Stephen King very famously argues that writing is hard work, whether best seller or Pulitzer Prize winning. By this standard, no one is "good" at science, art, or writing—even life.
- If you give up on new skills when they become hard, you will never become better. Contrary to intuition and popular belief, researchers like Henry L. Roediger III and Mark A. McDaniel have found that the struggle involved with learning difficult material and skills can actually make learners remember it more and be able to apply the ideas more widely. The one who struggles with the learning, but persists, will be able to retrieve that memory longer and across more situations.
- This idea doesn't value the discomfort of growing and learning new things. "I suck at this," "I don't read," and "I'm not a writer" are stories people tell themselves that keep them from believing in their ability to grow and allows them to opt out of continuing to be uncomfortable working on a skill.
- We can train ourselves and our students to *like* the challenge of difficult work, setting them up for a lifetime of learning and growing. Learning to enjoy the struggle makes for a happier and more successful life.

All of those standards systems—state, Common Core, Next Generation Science Standards—are based on the idea that the complex and abstract skills needed as adults can be broken down and taught step-by-step. Of course, the framing of all the testing and grades sends another message, but we'll get to that.

RESEARCH ON MASTERY AND COMPETENCE

The early intrinsic motivation researchers found that people painted, surfed, studied, and danced, not because of the money or fame rewards, but because mastering a skill provided a flow experience. Mihaly Csikszentmihalyi, the primary investigator of flow, defined it as an autotelic experience "rewarding in and of itself." Competence, another term for mastery in the intrinsic motivation research, "is a prerequisite to flow," according to psychologist Richard Mitchell. "Competence grows from the process of recognizing one's abilities and applying them meaningfully and completely.... Competence emerges when a person's talent, skills, and resources find useful application in meeting a commensurate challenge, problem, or difficulty," Mitchell writes in his book *Mountain Experience: The Psychology and Sociology of Adventure*.

Solving a Rubik's cube, rock climbing, sudoku, writing a sestina or acrostic poem, revising a personal statement to get it under five hundred words, finding meaning in "The Love Song of J. Alfred Prufrock," and mastering new and difficult skills make us feel alive. Finding a way to nurture—and not extinguish—that exhilaration in the classroom is the work of good teaching. Work from Edward Deci and Richard Ryan with self-determination theory prompted researchers to study workplaces and schools and found despite what might be intuitive, easy work wasn't the most enjoyable.

Instead, students and workers were more motivated to keep working and were happier when their tasks were in the sweet spot—challenging but doable. If you've ever worked a mindless job, you would understand the findings of Maria Allison and Margaret Carlisle Duncan, who found that boring work was one of the top stressors for unskilled women laborers. Not having enough to do or tasks that don't engage can actually stress people. Good news: that's never going to happen to teachers themselves. Teachers can modify assignments and allow personalization, so students can always be working toward their next reading, writing, and speaking goal. Making learning goals transparent and having kids learn to set their own learning goals increases buy-in and relevance in schools. Students need coaching in setting short-term, achievable, and moderately challenging goals, according to psychologist Edwin Locke in his thirty-five-year investigation into effective goal setting.

GETTING UNCOMFORTABLE

Instantaneous downloading of apps, celebrities who claim that schools should resemble game shows, and a culture that wants schools to entertain all miss the point that learning—rewiring the brain in a way that sticks over time and helps a child feel competent—takes work. That's how those neural pathways are laid down and reinforced to be accessed again. We are not computers that can download a new software in a moment, while snazzy little animations do handstands to entertain. Learning is work.

Please do not misunderstand; learners need positive feelings about school. As Barbara Fredrickson postulates with her "broaden and build" research, positive emotions allow humans to grow emotionally and cognitively. Students need to feel safe and cared for at school for optimal learning. But transmitting the value that school should be a variety show of special effects and charm that can be passively enjoyed negates the purpose of learning and the reality that humans need struggle to learn. Instead, educators have an opportunity to teach kids to struggle—and like it. As Winston Churchill said, "Continuous effort—not strength or intelligence—is the key to unlocking our key potential."

Educators have the job of making that continuous effort enjoyable. A physically and emotionally safe school culture is the first step. The next step is allowing students to get uncomfortable cognitively. The goal is to be emotionally comfortable and intellectually uncomfortable.

Strength-based researchers like Martin Seligman explain how individual strengths like love or honesty facilitate positive feelings of self and are thus intrinsically motivating and can aid in finding success in other areas. Bella may have a problem with finishing her reading homework, but she values her perseverance in finishing the mile run; explaining to her that reading takes the same kind of perseverance may suggest to her a strength she can use. So schooling can connect kids to their strengths. When students feel positive about themselves as learners, they can take risks and try new things. Those emotional tools make the cognitive effort possible.

Educators can create classrooms and schools where the effort of learning is celebrated, where students and staff breathe through the toil of learning. Many elementary and middle schools celebrate pages read in public graphs; that's celebrating mastery and effort. Honor rolls work too. But school culture changes when we also celebrate the mastery of students who aren't the best students but are doing their best. Those schools have taught all students to celebrate mastery at all levels.

WHERE FAILURE IS A SAFE PLACE

How many times as adults do you write something important and not get a chance to revise? (Heck, I occasionally have people preread regular emails because sometimes my writing sucks.) Professional writers stress that their best writing comes from revising skunky drafts. If they didn't write badly, they wouldn't write at all. Yet high-stakes testing and writing, exit exams, Scholastic Achievement Test (SAT), Advanced Placement (AP), district assessments, and Smarter Balance testing make failure a big deal. It's hard to experiment with new vocabulary, writing techniques, or reading strategies when so much hangs in the balance, but that's where learning happens.

We can't eliminate high-stakes testing, but we can model real-world writing and the writing process the rest of the time in our classrooms, which means we have to not only allow failure but encourage it as well. We should tell our students that we want to see them fail occasionally, because if they don't fail sometimes, they aren't challenging themselves enough all of the time. This also means a portfolio system where students write often, but the majority of their grades come from a self-chosen portfolio of their own work that they've chosen how to revise, allowing them to learn to fail safely.

GOAL SETTING IN THE LITERACY CLASSROOM

Learners need goal setting explicitly taught and modeled until they can drive that tool themselves. The standards-based report cards and frequent parent conferences often seen in lower grades are handy places to begin the important process of asking students to take part in discussions about their academic mastery and goal setting. The trick is that these assessments have to be seen as capturing a snapshot of past learning to discover where a student should focus next and students need help choosing goals small enough to be achievable and breaking larger goals into smaller chunks. Even kindergarteners can be asked to explain how they've improved based on work samples months apart and clearly explain their growing mastery and next steps. Portfolios, for all ages, allow students to see their mastery over time.

It's easy to take today's skills for granted, but evidence of increasing competency when the daily growth wasn't noticeable reminds learners of the importance of practice and perseverance for their next goals. In primary classrooms, teachers keep large folders of student work to prepare report cards. In classrooms of older children, it may make sense for the students to place work in the portfolios or even to have two portfolios, a working portfolio for their current writing and a cumulative portfolio for their work across time.

Many schools are keeping multi-year portfolios of student work as a powerful way to show students their mastery over longer periods of time. Some teachers have gone to digital portfolios as well, which is especially useful if formative and casual writing is kept alongside the larger published assessments. Conferences allow for student–teacher meetings to discuss mastery and coach goal setting, and can be formal or informal depending on the teacher and classroom.

Research by Mary Ann Smith and the National Writing Project illustrates that conferences and portfolio systems can be very effective in shaping student thinking about mastery—as long as the systems are created by the teachers and change how teachers talk to students about mastery and growth. Systems forced on teachers from above that do not change the mindset of students and staff fail to change student perceptions or motivation. Read more about this from articles published by the National Writing Project from Violet Dickson, Shirley-Dale Easley, Kay Mitchell, Thomas Flynn, Mary King, Kathleen Jones, Douglas Kaufman, Monette McIver, Shelby Wolf, Mary Ann Smith, Sandra Murphy, Taejoon Park, and Jane Juska. Reading about other teachers' methods of discussing mastery with students can help you form the system that will work best for you.

MASTERY WITH DIFFERENT POPULATIONS

Gifted and Talented Education (GATE)

Gifted and talented, advanced learners, early finishers, higher-end students—whatever school districts or teachers, even within their own heads, call it—some students need some extra help with thinking in terms of mastery and competence because learning comes so easily to them that they sometimes miss that it's happening! These students have much to lose with fixed mindsets because being labeled smart in early grades can make them feel that they "get dumber" as they get older. Since many school subjects feel easy for them, they need help learning to persevere when they reach subjects or levels that feel hard. Keeping track of learning goals completed and how to work through difficulties keeps these early finishers engaged in the classroom and looking for new challenges, even as they reach harder topics.

Special Education

Promoting mastery for special education students has long been understood as important. Nancy Mather, Barbara J. Mendling, and Rhia Roberts' *Writing Assessment and Instruction for Students with Learning Disabilities* explains

Table 3.1. How to Teach Goal Setting for Different Ages

Age	Activity	Instructions	You say	Benefit
Pre-K, K	Pictograph checklist	During assessment, ask children to choose goals from assembled pictographs. At next assessment, ask them if they accomplished their goal or are still working on it.	What would you like to get better at next? Where would you like to grow? How have you worked toward your goals? What could you do to get better at that?	Young children benefit from hearing the explicit questions of goal setting and having the power for their goals put in their hands.
Primary	Goal board	On a chart in the classroom, have each child choose a public goal that is specific, like cleaning up after art without being asked for two weeks or getting a 90 percent or better on a month of spelling tests.	Are you working toward your goal? What could you do to achieve your goal? You did it! Erase and choose a new goal.	Public goal boards help create a culture of mastery. Students will often remind each other of their goals in a supportive way.
Elementary–middle school	Goal sticks	Ask kids what they want to learn or get better at doing. Write their goals on popsicle sticks stored with their name in the classroom. Periodically ask them which goal they are working on and how. When they achieve that goal, they get to write a new one. The finished goal sticks are marked and put back with the others.	What goal are you practicing for now? How are you working toward learning your goal? Which goal is that behavior supporting? Now that you've mastered this, what next?	This introduces the idea of juggling and mastering many goals. The finished goals serve as a reminder of the difficult skills they've already mastered, increasing confidence in their competence. During flexible time, they can choose one of their goals to work on quietly.

Middle school–high school	Grading period conferences	As teachers prepare report cards, they ask students to grade themselves and then conference about their goals and mastery.	Did you grow as much as you intended on this goal? What would mastery of this goal look like?	This asks students to critique their work and speculate how mastery would appear, higher-order thinking. Using gradual release of responsibility, these check-ins are less frequent than other methods.
High school	Portfolios	Students choose works to keep in a large folder to demonstrate mastery across genres and skills. Periodically, they write metacognitively about the evidence in the portfolio.	What reading and writing processes helped you achieve your goals? What did you learn about your revision process? How can you take what you learned about yourself into other parts of your life?	Increasing metacognition writing tasks brings relevance and another level of mastery—thinking to writing tasks. Studies on entry-level college English classes show that being able to write metacognitively about writing predicts college writing success.

> I use conferences and portfolios together in my high school classroom. Students keep most of their writing in their folder that they use almost every day in class. Their folder also is how we keep track of conference notes. We conference four times a year after they've written me a conference letter explaining where they've grown in reading, writing, speaking, and thinking. During the conference, I take notes on the inside of their folder until they take over that responsibility after some practice.
>
> - Conferences start with the question: What are your concerns about life and school right now? Since the conferences are fast, 5–10 minutes while other kids are reading, revising, or writing, it's tempting to skip this question. But they can't focus on discussing their academic vocabulary in reflective writing when they need to tell you they've recently become homeless or need surgery or got in their dream school and are desperate for scholarships.
> - Question 2: How have you grown in reading, writing, speaking, or thinking? The language implies that those skills can be grown even though many enter the classroom thinking their communication, reading, and thinking skills are set. Students who can't come up with anything—our culture prohibits academic bragging—get a mark that they should work on metacognition in their folder and a small teaching moment. Understanding strengths, personally and academically, allows for more accurate assessment and confidence in mastery, and it provides platforms from which to work on weaknesses.
> - Question 3: What would you like to work on next in reading, writing, speaking, or thinking? This question not only implies ever-growing mastery on these skills but also makes the choice of goals theirs.
> - Question 4: What do you need from me to achieve those goals? This puts the teacher in role of coach and the student in charge of goals. Since I coach and provide tips for working on their next goals when we discuss Question 3, I usually get only small concrete requests here, like a book to review grammar, or a letter of recommendation, or more practice with public speaking.
>
> After the first conference of the year, after Question 2, I put them to work finding samples from their folder showing growth on our concerns from the previous conferences while I read their letter and transcribe their thoughts into the conference notes on the inside of the folder. They get to check off and date the notes from previous conferences where they mastered those previous goals. They use all of the conference letters and conference notes in the inside of their folders to write their portfolio cover letters at the end of each semester explaining their growth with samples.

how breaking down skills into manageable chunks gives students mastery and confidence in learning new material. The art of goal setting with special education students, using *Individualized Education Programs* (IEPs) or more informal checklists, should happen often and collaboratively to help students who struggle to own their learning. Feeling disenfranchised from the school system not only colors emotionally their experience but also takes ownership of their learning from school away from them. Their slower mastery can leave them feeling defensive and bitter, but a whole school culture focused on learning from failure and setting personal goals can soothe the sting of self-doubt of slower learning.

English Language Learners

Learning a new language comes stealthily. In an immersive classroom, speaking gains creep up so fast, yet gradually, that students may feel that their learning is standing still but actually be much improved. Videotaped presentations, peer-graded conversations with a supportive classroom culture, self-assessment with read-aloud lists, and metacognitive self-assessment tools can all help them see their growing mastery. More elusive goals, like preposition use, benefit from more long-range mastery aids like portfolios.

WRITING IS HARD WORK

From writer's chair to writing workshops, teachers have the difficult task of helping students see themselves as writers and discovering that writing is hard work. There's a myth in our society that writers are born with a gift and that most of us will never be writers. With the advent of the Internet, self-publishing, and increased instruction and expectation in writing for readers, most students will have published their writing in some form during their lifetime, even if it's just Internet comments. That increased purpose of writing comes with increased mastery goals. Organizations like the National Writing Project and its sites in every state and U.S. territory, the National Council of Teachers of English, various teacher unions, and education systems have made huge strides in teaching mastery and mastery strategies like portfolios, conferencing, writers' workshop, digital publishing, breaking down the writing process, and peer review.

Good literacy curricula, the Common Core Literacy standards or the Expository Reading and Writing Curriculum (ERWC), should be recursive—that is, keep coming back to the same topics to make them more complex and incorporate skills learned later. Most people learn to write a paragraph in second grade, three sentences of simple vocabulary on a single topic. By eighth grade, they've learned to explore more abstract topics with more academic vocabulary. Imagine if students didn't also learn new types of paragraphs like introductions or summary or dialogue or new paragraph strategies, but were stuck with the same three-sentence model from second grade. Mastery in literacy must be recursive. Writing skill is on a continuum, and mastery is when students keep moving along it.

Instructors who have not yet shown classes their own writing and how it moves along that continuum with work and revision miss out on an important teaching moment. Teachers may feel self-conscious that their students may surpass their skills or worry that more advanced writing will intimidate the young writers. Both are probably true. Teaching mastery means facing both of those ideas and framing them in lessons to the class focused on increasing writing mastery growth for everyone, even adults.

READING IS HARD WORK

Reading assessment and goal setting, even without student input, happen regularly in the lower grades. Primary teachers, knowing they're responsible for teaching reading and reading strategies, devote instructional time to the explicit teaching of reading mastery. However, there is a perception from teachers and students alike that older students already know how to read and there's not much to be taught there. As Stephen Reder published in *Perspectives on Language and Literacy*, adults continue to make slow but steady growth in reading and reading strategies throughout their working lives. Put another way: the idea that high schoolers read as well as they're going to is silly. (I read better than I did in high school, and so do you.) The only adults who see a stagnation or decline in reading are the ones who stop trying to get better at it.

Does your classroom have a reading contest? The California ERWC includes a unit written by the lovely Mira-Lisa Katz that encourages students to perceive themselves as reader experts on a variety of tasks. It might be counterintuitive to media coverage about teens and reading, but today's kids read more than previous generations between their messaging, reading on their phones and newsfeeds, not to mention, their love of literature.

Acknowledging their expertise with different kinds of texts—dirt biking magazines, music, music lyrics, calculus texts, and video game cheat sheets—helps them see themselves as readers that are varying strategies, working on mastery, experts on some types of reading, and growing in others. As recent research has pointed out, reading, for all ages, increases feelings of competency and life satisfaction. Experiences, especially those that build competency, provide more feelings of happiness than products.

TEACHER MASTERY: AN EVER-MOVING TARGET AS WELL

Teachers need to teach mastery. But teacher mastery has become political. Schools and governments have the reasonable idea that, as professionals, teachers should have ongoing learning and mastery. As educators, we would never design a curriculum that makes our students feel powerless, obscures the end goals, disenfranchises them from the goal-setting process, or takes away their identity as learners. Teacher-proof curricula or teacher scripts do that to teachers. Humans are designed to learn. Go learn.

Chinese-U.S. foreign policy, Spanish, mosaic art, chess, woodworking—these might not translate into your curriculum, but they will show your students your willingness to learn something new. Through unions, bargaining units, and relationships within your schools, push for teacher-chosen professional development and goal setting. We know it works for kids, for Fortune 500 companies; it's the right thing for teachers to do and model. Teachers know their students and classroom needs better than anyone else.

I know where I could use more knowledge or skills. I'm always looking for more strategies to teach students to persevere in difficult reading or learn to revise for strength. I keep an eye for ways to grow those skills, and my principal supports my seeking mastery and encourages staff to share our learning with each other. Modeling for students should include that intellectual curiosity and willingness to be uncomfortable learning new things.

TEACHERS AND WRITERS TALK ABOUT COMPETENCE, MASTERY, AND GOAL SETTING

To set goals, we keep asking, starting in kindergarten even, "You've gone this far. What's your next goal?" By the time they're second graders, they've internalized that process and will tell us at the end of a project, "I learned this, and next project I'll work on this." Fourth graders and older are invited to conferences to explain the evidence of their mastery to their parents. When school is about meeting their own learning goals, they want to come, they want to learn.

—Lisa Jager

About Lisa: Lisa Jager, the principal of Redwood Preparatory Charter School in Humboldt County, California, has designed a system K–8 where students are involved in their own educational goals.

Take-away: Teaching kids goal setting from young ages changes their purpose. Putting mastery in their hands makes school and learning more meaningful. When school is a place students know they can meet their intrinsic needs for competency, they never develop the idea that school doesn't matter or that their real lives are somewhere else.

I'm very transparent about lessons, what I'm trying to get out of it so they're part of the learning process. No magic tricks. And I'm very lucky because I get to have kids two years in a row and sometimes three and sometimes four, so we're able to do reflection about how they were and how they are. It's good to have those discussions with them because that's where they really learn and really finds what works for them. Transparency is so important. If they are struggling with finding a thesis, they have to be part of the conversation. It's a conversation because it's their learning and they're in charge of their mastery.

—Gini Wozny

About Gini: Gini Wozny is an English teacher at Academy of the Redwoods, an early college high school in Humboldt County, California.

Take-away: Wozny exemplifies the role of teacher as writing and reading coach, helping students find their goals and coaching their incremental mastery of the content. At her school, teachers often have students over several years so they can help coach them to their learning goals. An unusual philosophy for a high school, but Academy of the Redwoods' teachers coach, or advise, their students while they attend college classes as high school students.

Teachers are amazing when it comes to educational triage. Interacting with so many students with so many diverse needs in such a limited amount of time means that teachers must be master managers of human dynamics and the micropolitics that exist within classroom and school environments. They must have a strong sense of "withitness," meaning that they must be aware of everything going on in their classrooms at all times. This also means that they must anticipate potential issues, they must read facial expressions, body posture, tone of voice, and myriad other subtle cues. In short, one important attribute of effective teachers is knowing and valuing people and their needs and perspectives. Coupling this with pedagogical effectiveness—knowing how to deliver content in meaningful and comprehensible ways that are compelling and memorable, knowing how and when to appropriately differentiate, knowing how to check for understanding, and in essence, knowing how to engage students—takes a high degree of skill and often many years of experience. Effective teachers reach a state of flow when they are able to navigate the complex interplay of classroom management, content, instruction, assessment, social nuances, and numerous other facets of the teaching and learning process. This is much harder to do than what is visible on the surface (and especially to the untrained and inexperienced eye), and it is much harder to measure than many evaluation tools are capable.

—David Bosso

About David: Dr. David Bosso argues that the challenge of teaching fuels teachers' intrinsic motivation in the classroom.

Take-away: Being transparent with students about enjoying the challenge of teaching models how to lean into difficult work and enjoy growing as learners. Students benefit not only from the additional expertise that teachers get when they keep learning but also from seeing that adults are still learning and growing, and that seeking mastery can be exciting and fun and never-ending.

LEARN MORE

What to Read

- Csikszentmihalyi, Mihaly, and Isabella Selega Csikszentmihalyi. *Optimal Experience: Psychological Studies of Flow in Consciousness*. Cambridge: Cambridge University Press, 1988. Print.

    This collection of studies addresses the concept of flow from many angles, working women, Japanese motorcycle gangs, and international school comparisons.
- Dickson, Violet M. *The Transfer and Sustainability of a School-Wide Writing Program: Year 2*. Diss. Web. June 26, 2013. http://udini.proquest.com/view/the-transfer-and-sustainability-of-goid:818469083/.

    This study published by the National Writing Project discusses the inherent problems in top-down writing programs with portfolios.
- Easley, Shirley-Dale, and Kay Mitchell. *Portfolios Matter: What, Where, When, Why and How to Use Them*. Markham: Pembroke, 2003. Print.

    An excellent practical guide to hows and whys of using portfolios and conferencing with elementary school students. Many practical tips and handouts to use in the process.
- Fountas, Irene C., and Gay Su Pinnell. *Teaching for Comprehending and Fluency: Thinking, Talking, and Writing about Reading, K–8*. Portsmouth, NH: Heinemann, 2006. Print.

    This book creates a continuum of literacy skills, partially inspiring the Common Core literacy standards. A chart in the book, "A Language and Literacy Framework for Literature and the Content Areas (K–8)," succinctly lays out how skills build mastery and can be found online.
- Flynn, Thomas, and Mary King. *Dynamics of the Writing Conference: Social and Cognitive Interaction*. Urbana, IL: National Council of Teachers of English, 1993. Print.

    This research into the cross-curricular evidence of higher-level thinking due to conferences explains the pathways to learning of conferences, especially relevant in light of Common Core.
- Graves, Donald H., and Bonnie S. Sunstein. *Portfolio Portraits*. Portsmouth, NH: Heinemann, 1992. Print.

    Stories from different levels of classrooms and administrators illustrate the many ways to use portfolios.

- Jones, Kathleen. "Portfolio Assessment as an Alternative to Grading Student Writing." 255–63. Colorado State. Web. 2013. http://wac.colostate.edu/books/tchudi/chapter18.pdf.

  One teacher's experience compares portfolio assessment to standard grading of writing.
- Kaufman, Douglas. *Conferences & Conversations: Listening to the Literate Classroom*. Portsmouth, NH: Heinemann, 2000. Print.

  This book addresses using portfolios and conferencing in the classroom as a method of professional and personal growth of the teacher.
- King, Stephen. *On Writing: A Memoir of the Craft*. New York, NY: Scribner, 2000. Print.

  The American novelist has written 54 works that have sold 350 million copies and argues that all writers, even bestselling ones, have to practice and work to get better.
- Mather, Nancy, Barbara J. Mendling, and Rhia Roberts. "Writing Assessment and Instruction for Students with Learning Disabilities." *Google Books*. Hoboken, NJ: John Wiley & Sons, 2009. Web. Feb. 18, 2015.

  This book, aimed at special education teachers, repeatedly stresses the need for the feeling of mastery, especially for learners who have been academically unsuccessful before.
- McIver, Monette C., and Shelby A. Wolf. *Writing Conferences: Powerful Tools for Writing Instruction*. Rep. no. 494. Boulder: University of Colorado, 1998. Center for Research on Evaluation, Standards, and Student Testing. Web. 2013. https://www.cse.ucla.edu/products/reports/TECH494.pdf.

  This case study of one Kentucky classroom explains conferencing used to prepare for the state portfolio assessments.
- Murphy, Sandra, and Mary Ann Smith. *Writing Portfolios: A Bridge from Teaching to Assessment*. Scarborough, Ontario: Pippin Corporation, 1992. Print.

  This good practical guide to creating portfolios follows students through high school, with both anecdotal and quantitative data.
- Park, Taejoon. "An Overview of Portfolio-based Writing Assessment." *The Forum* 4.2. New York, NY: Teachers College, Columbia University. Web. June 26, 2013. http://www.tc.columbia.edu/academic/tesol/WJFiles/pdf/TaejoonParkForum.pdf.

  This survey of the history of portfolio use gives definitions, advantages, and disadvantages of portfolios found in the literature.
- Seligman, Martin E. P. *Flourish: A Visionary New Understanding of Happiness and Well-being*. New York, NY: Free, 2011. Print.

Seligman, former president of the American Psychological Association and researcher, details positive emotion research, strength-based research, and application of those ideas to realms of life.
- Smith, Mary Ann, and Jane Juska. *The Whole Story: Teachers Talk about Portfolios*. Berkeley, CA: National Writing Project, 2001. Print.

  A range of essays, with the perspective of a decade of portfolios, this book discusses what works and what does not with portfolios.
- Top 20 Principles from Psychology for PreK–12 Teaching and Learning. APA Report. Washington, DC: American Psychological Association, 2015. Web.

  The report's Principle 12 explains the need for students to value learning that does not come easily, and the report argues repeatedly for learning that is repeated, incremental, and attached to prior learning.

Chapter Four

Autonomy and Gamification
Choose Your Own Adventure

It is our choices ... that show what we truly are, far more than our abilities.

—J. K. Rowling

According to decades of research and large meta-analyses in psychology, business, and education, autonomy—the feeling of control over our lives and choices—gives our lives positive emotions, feelings of competency, and allows us to work harder and longer. It's a simple concept with far-reaching ramifications.

A cliché in our culture, disliking school, can often be explained simply by the lack of control our students feel over their day. Structured times for snack and math, seating charts, school uniforms, required writing topics, assigned books, and selected peer sets for group work: school systems choose children's learning, socialization, and physical environment. Do you know an incredibly intelligent and driven individual who didn't do well in school? When asked why, they usually offer some variation on the idea that they didn't get to study what truly interested them.

RESEARCH: LOCUS OF CONTROL, LEARNED HELPLESSNESS, AND AUTONOMY

As Julian Rotter first proposed in the 1950s, and Bernard Weiner and others have further expanded and developed since, locus of control explains whether people feel they have control over their lives. In general, people who perceive themselves as having an internal locus of control, in charge of the events of their lives, report less stress and more motivation for continued growth and effort.

For example, Rotter used a pen-and-paper quiz to determine if subjects externalized or internalized the causes around them. Locus of control changes with our life experience, but an internal locus of control can be an accurate predictor of high school and college graduation rates, recovery rates from illness, and volunteerism.

Lack of choice and control can create a long-lasting lens of the world that says events happen without the ability to shape them or respond to them, or, as Martin Seligman coined, "learned helplessness." This external locus of control stresses people physically and emotionally and makes them less likely to try to change their environment. It can create a self-defeating cycle that disempowers children or adults.

Children, of course, need guidance and support from adults, but the more teachers and families let students make choices, the more invested in their own futures students become. The self-determination theorists studying education would tell us what most parents of toddlers already know: If you want a child to try something new, from canned peaches to writing a persuasive essay, letting them choose from appropriate examples is the quickest way to

Table 4.1. Giving Supportive Choices

You say ...	Try saying ...	Because ...
Do you think you can handle that more difficult choice?	This topic may be more difficult than this topic, but the choice is yours.	Students lose motivation when they think their teacher doubts their ability but can handle more difficult tasks when they intersect with their interests. Topic selection can help students grow skills (Deci).
When you show me that you can handle looser deadlines, you won't have to do all of the drafts.	What kind of process do you think would be best for you to do your best work on this assignment?	Counterintuitively, learners may be conditioned to being controlled and act in ways that seem to require it, but those students need the choices to develop autonomy even more than students who enter the classroom as more autonomous (Deci).
There are several choices of readings, but you should choose the one that matches your reading level.	Choose the readings for this assignment from the list.	Controlling choices defeats the goal of choices: autonomy. Also, synthesizing from several sources of different reading levels requires students to compare information and purpose, a more sophisticated skill (Common Core Framework).

success. Immunization schedules, city curfews, class times, and the cafeteria menu may still be chosen without their input, but classrooms should provide choices where possible.

As Edward Deci and Richard Ryan have found since their work in the late 1980s, no one—be it students or employees—likes being controlled. Fellow high school teacher Raven Coit explains it this way: "The more I feel controlled, the less ownership I take of the process and the results. I withdraw from responsibility. I'm far more likely to be creative and take risks if the process and the results are mine to be proud of. And so are my students."

Deci and Ryan have assayed various wordings, deliveries, and populations to describe the effect of controlling language on even simple instructions. Not only choices offered but also how they are offered seems to affect feelings of autonomy and intrinsic motivation.

As Jasmine D. Williams, psychologist in Education at University of Pittsburgh, and her colleagues argue, choice can be accomplished in the classroom in a variety of ways—"pace, format, topic, and mobility"—and dramatically affects student engagement.

GAMIFICATION OF LEARNING

Game designers and proponents of gamification like Thomas Malone discuss autonomy as agency, the ability to decide your direction and goals. Malone's work spawned decades of research into how the principles of good video game design could increase credit card use, make games more addicting, and coerce education into becoming more engaging.

There's been much talk in the last few years about gamification of learning, like adding levels and cartoon characters to drill worksheets will make education more inherently rewarding. Those strategies aren't always successful because unless all of those levels and sparkle are attached to actual choice and autonomy, with meaningful mastery of ever-increasing skill, the gamification is hollow.

Humans find games rewarding because games are a form of learning, and educators can use good game design to inform teaching and learning. For one, games aren't high stakes. It never happens in a game that you get one chance to learn a skill, and if you don't master the skill, you're out of the game. In games, each turn has multiple lives and you can try each level as many times as it takes for you to learn it.

Education can be like that too, without the shame or labeling of remediation or tutoring. Games allow you to keep score against yourself. If teachers are the only people in the classroom who own the goal setting, students can't enjoy the game of leveling up as much. Also, too often we take for granted in education that students are getting stronger and faster at important skills. When we don't make their progress explicit, they often miss their own improvement. And that's a missed opportunity. When students see their progress, they believe in their own growth and ability to learn the hard stuff, whatever the next "hard stuff" will be.

Excellent video games also have a story that draws the player through the game: a reason to play, characters to rescue, a mission to complete. When we make the purpose of our classroom and curriculum more explicit, we invite students to be part of a larger and more engaging story, ideally the stories of their futures. Finding their purpose and seeking new levels of competency are less likely to happen, though, if teachers don't give students choices about goals, points of views, and texts.

Most importantly, games allow learners to explore choices and the effects of their choices. Too often, gamification in schools doesn't allow for student choice or autonomy, a key reason for engagement in video games. It might be tempting to include elaborate leveling and award systems to motivate students, but the first step is giving them more choice in what they read, what they write about what they read, and how and when they accomplish those tasks.

PACE, ORDER, AND PROCESS

"Deadlines, imposed goals, and surveillance" all decrease intrinsic motivation for tasks, according to psychology researcher Edward Deci. It's such a quandary for teachers. If there are no deadlines, students may not feel the push to work and grow, and then what do we assess for report cards? Especially in teaching reading and writing, the first draft might not be the best draft. We all need to revise. How can teachers emphasize writing process without letting students do multiple drafts?

Common Core stresses process, and that looks like different things for different people. Your process might look like research, reflectively write, research, reflectively write, steep, then outline all at once, flesh out details, write the easy stuff and go back to the harder stuff when you know more. Maybe there is walking and dancing and teaching between all of these steps? That's your process. So a timed essay on a prompt never seen before? Yep, you might be able to regurgitate the lecture into an organized statement, but not create.

Some students have a similar process; most have their own best practices for writing well. Ease of tasks in the writing process varies from student to student; so should pacing.

There are many solutions to the pacing problem, including portfolios, checklists, and inverse grading.

Portfolios allow students to choose what's graded and to revise those works until they are ready to be graded and focus on producing fewer works of higher quality. They can be done digitally or hard copy or combined and sometimes integrate features of the checklist or inverted grading.

> When I've used checklists before, the lists would show the minimum standards to be met for each letter grade for that grading period. For example, perhaps for a "D" a student would have to produce a persuasive essay, a reflective essay, two expository reports, and a persuasive speech 3–5 minutes long. Each assignment would have to be revised multiple times until it was proficient for grade level. This style of classroom design again focuses on doing fewer assignments with more competence. Students enjoyed having a clear-cut list of expectations for the grading period and knowing what to expect. The downside was that some students aimed low for their grade goal and the backward planning required the teacher to know every assessment for the grading period before it began.

Checklists, on the other hand, consist of skills listed in the standards, that students can show any time during the grading period.

Inverse grading is a system inspired by video game scoring. Every student starts with zero points and continues to add points for showing skills and growth as the grading period continues. As they complete assignments at their own pace, teachers act as coaches and guides. This works particularly well with a flipped classroom, but no matter how achieved requires teachers to front load all of the instructional materials and videos before the grading period begins. All of these put the pacing of when assignments are done in the students' hands, allowing them more choice.

FORMAT

As Thomas Armstrong writes in *Multiple Intelligences in the Classroom*, students show us their preferred format of learning and assessment in their behavior in the classroom. While it doesn't make sense to substitute writing for carving wood, or replace reading with watching videos, sometimes it makes sense in the literacy classroom to have students choose their preferred format.

For instance, a speaking presentation could allow students to choose their visuals from hand-drawn posters, computer animation, or three-dimensional visualization, working from their strengths. When the goal is display of content knowledge, the format of display can play to the student's preference.

Students can also be coached to use their stronger intelligences to augment the weaker formats for them. For example, people with strong visual strengths can find note-taking from lectures or oral instructions difficult as they are distracted by their own writing of the material. Using their strength

Table 4.2. Writing Topics and Choice

Example	Stance	Subject	Ancillary focus
Third-grade biography	Who was more important to our country, Abraham Lincoln or George Washington?	Choose from this list of hundred famous Americans for your report.	Choose a famous American pioneer in your favorite school subject like art or science.
Middle school report of information	Which invention from the Middle Ages changed life the most?	Choose from this list of topics from the Middle Ages.	Consider your science fair topic this year. How would this issue have been discussed in the Middle Ages?
Of Mice and Men literary analysis	What should George have done at the end of the novel?	Consider the idea of discrimination from one of the characters' point of view.	Choose a related topic from what you have learned about American history this year and do a historical analysis of the novel.

of visual processing, they should watch the speaker, instead of taking notes or taking notes without looking—tricky!—and write the notes after the lecture from memory. Alternatively, writers who work best from an outline can make a minisketch to guide them through a shorter write.

TOPIC

Writing is so personal that it's difficult, especially for the beginning writers, to write against their own thoughts or beliefs. Choice of writing or speaking topic can be accomplished by giving options in stance, subject, or ancillary focus. This autonomy improves motivation and engagement in writing, according to teacher and writer Nancie Atwell and others.

MOBILITY

Where do your students work? Are they allowed to move around? Can they choose where they write? Today a student asked to sit on the floor for her hour of writing on her personal statement for college. Her class had been working on increased writing perseverance, but choosing her position made her more comfortable and productive. Allowing that choice reinforced to her classmates that learning and respect of each other are more important than ideas about controlling student mobility.

A local elementary school moves to a common area for reading and writing time, and students find a comfy place to read or write or practice spelling words. Of course, with some traditional educational models, this is difficult to accomplish. Many elementary schools have couches and rugs and dedicated reading spaces, and students report higher enjoyment of reading in those grades.

Most language classrooms, through high school, have bookcases, but perhaps literacy teachers should consider more comfortable furnishings as well. More is at stake than their comfort. Students learn that reading and writing do not just happen in desks; there are as many ways to do it as there are books to read and pieces to write.

CHOICE OF READINGS

Nelson Graff and other researchers have written and argued for more student choice in readings. The data comparing primary school students to high school students in reading engagement prove clearly that students enjoy works that they pick out more than works that are selected for them. Of course, teachers want students to choose challenging reading levels and important texts, but self-chosen reading topics are an excellent way to practice more difficult reading skills. It's easier to stretch in vocabulary or understanding complex structure if the reader is interested in the topic.

Teachers want to assign texts that inform the writing and works that add to the writing dialog, but a balance can be struck by offering students choices from a reading list of appropriate works. Teachers can act as a reading coach for student-selected reading goals, or require some form of reading logs for students.

Table 4.3. What Does Choice of Reading Look Like in the Different Grades?

Primary school	*Middle school*	*High school*
Good fit books in the CAFE system	Reading workshop	Literature circles
Reading logs	Book groups	Book talks
	Reading conferences	Book reviews
		Reading choice boards

IMPLICATIONS FOR COURSE DESIGN

So how do we design courses that give students choices in order to encourage them to keep trying and leveling up and make learning fun again? There's no single answer: whether it's portfolios, transforming the points structure so that they begin with zeroes and have unlimited ability to enter work and grow the grade they want, or employing checklists of mastery skills.

Unfortunately, students who seem to not be able to handle choices need them the most. The research has found since the beginning, with psychologist Martin Seligman, that people who have experienced a lack of control or choice in their life cease to expect it or know what to do with it. What he called "learned helplessness," and later Edward Deci and Richard Ryan described as wanting control, results from people coming from environments that control and limit choices. As much as teachers may be tempted to limit choices for those students until they show they can handle choices, or even want them, the research suggests that instead students should have more choices than they want as long as they still feel safe.

Some clues that students do not feel safe with their autonomy includes crying when faced with college application choices, begging for teacher-selected writing prompts, or over reliance on teacher feedback or conferencing, needing almost daily reassurance. Weaning them off these controls may be harder than for autonomous students and take more time, but it is even more important than with students who are already self-directed.

TEACHERS AND WRITERS TALK ABOUT THE IMPORTANCE OF CHOICE

I believe the 0 to 100 grading is one way to do it. But also giving the class collective goals, or heck, make teams in the class for competitive goals. Students not only need a more interactive classroom, but a team-oriented one as well because usually people have to work together in the workforce of today and school is all about preparing them for the future. This will make them also want to progress together with students that have an easier time learning or helping those that don't, so that they all will reach their class goal. Lastly give the students freedom with their work, in English let students write short stories using the things they learn. Let math students create problems for others to solve. Learning things through actions is much easier than learning through looking at words on a paper.

—*Alex Sanborn*

About Alex: Alex Sanborn is currently my student, but he also writes a blog about gamification, Psychology in Games, that explores how video games use psychology to be more engaging. He explained how gamification principles could be used in the classroom, from a student's perspective.

Take-away: Students involved with video gaming already expect and understand the concepts of gamification: choice of game play and pacing, being a part of a game community or good story, the opportunity to reach for increasing mastery with multiple chances, and the growth mindset of enjoying a challenge. Integrating those ideas into the classroom not only uses ideas they already intuitively understand from video games, but makes learning and education more engaging for them.

> *I feel the best way is to use some of Thomas Armstrong's ideas, based on the multiple intelligences. Specifically, provide students with options/choices to show the teacher/classmates what was learned. Based on the multiple intelligences, assignments can culminate in musical performances, computer graphics, a variety of written formats, including songs, poetry, interview segments, etc. Open up choice on the response options and students will feel more motivated and engaged, and will also be more responsive to efforts to address their deficiencies—through their strengths.*
>
> —*Dr. Maurice J. Elias*

About Maurice: Dr. Maurice J. Elias, professor of psychology at Rutgers University, is the academic director of the Collaborative, Rutgers' Center for Community-Based Research and Service and the coordinator for Improving School Climate for Academic and Life Success at Rutgers Center for Applied Psychology.

Take-away: Choice of presentation of learning allows students' learning to be personal and meaningful to them while still meeting content standards. Strengths-based learning allows all students to access the lesson from their different viewpoints and strengths.

> *We talk about choice a lot. It's about making choices. It's so empowering, it gives them autonomy. Like, "I made a choice that wasn't the greatest, and I can make a different choice tomorrow."*
>
> *They have lots of choice in writing. I have to have a book that everybody's reading because I have to provide the book. Books are about seminars. They can hate a book, they can love a book. As long as they can back it up with evidence. That takes growth and time. And I see that growth from their first year seminars to their second seminars.*
>
> *Revision in writing is a large part of their autonomy. If they want to be done with it they can be, or they can revise. Writing every day and then getting to choose the pieces they're graded on and develop mean they care more about their writing than when I assign essays.*
>
> —*Gini Wozny*

About Gini: Gini Wozny teaches at the Early College high school Academy of the Redwoods in Humboldt County, California, and I'm lucky to be her colleague.

Take-away: The choice of prompt, stance, and pieces to develop for their portfolio acknowledges that reading and writing is recursive, not linear. Professional writers write every day and come back to pieces as needed; providing the everyday discipline and allowing the freedom to make choices means students think of themselves as writers.

> *Students here have choice over where they work, choice over topics, whether they take it to a finished piece or just let it go. And a choice to show to others or not.*
>
> *—Melanie Downing*

About Melanie: Melanie Downing teaches sixth grade at Redwood Preparatory School in Fortuna, California.

Take-away: Her students use a combination of journaling for writing every day and idea generation, and blogs and projects to publish their best work to receive feedback and connect to their purposes.

LEARN MORE

What to Read

- Armstrong, Thomas. *Multiple Intelligences in the Classroom*. Alexandria, VA: Association for Supervision and Curriculum Development, 1994. Print.
  Armstrong's classic work explains student strengths and how teachers can tap into those strengths to increase student comfort in the classroom. He also suggests that acknowledging that all learners have strengths allows us to ask students to use those strengths to address their weaknesses as learners more effectively.
- Atwell, Nancie. *In the Middle: Writing, Reading, and Learning with Adolescents*. Upper Montclair, NJ: Boynton/Cook, 1987. Print.
  This classic text, revised in 2014 with a third edition, makes the case for choice in middle school reading and writing.
- Deci, Edward L., and Richard Flaste. *Why We Do What We Do: Understanding Self-motivation*. New York, NY: Penguin, 1996. Print.
  Deci's book explains the principles of self-determination theory in greater detail.
- Deci, Edward, and Richard Ryan. "The Support of Autonomy and the Control of Behavior." *Journal of Personality and Social Psychology* 53.6 (1987): 1024–37. Web.

This early paper in self-determination theory proposes that controlling other peoples' behavior leads to less intrinsic motivation of the controlled. People want to control their own lives and make their own choices.

- Smith, Anna. "No. Don't Surrender. Leverage." Blog post. *Developing Writers*. Jan. 16, 2015. Web. https://developingwriters.org/2015/01/16/no-dont-surrender-leverage-creativity-in-scholarly-work/#more-3501.

This blog explores the writing and research of graduate students in communication fields. As they write the thesis papers that consume their lives, they reflect on writing processes and research.

- Hamari, Juho, Jonna Koivisto, and Harri Sarsa. "Does Gamification Work? A Literature Review of Empirical Studies on Gamification." Proceedings of 47th Hawaii International Conference on System Sciences, Jan. 6–9, 2014. *IEEE Xplore Digital Library* (2014): 3025–34. Web. Apr. 2, 2016.

This survey of gamification research shows its current popularity but also highlights its limitations according to the research.

- Hunter, Jeremy, and Mihaly Csikszentmihalyi. "The Positive Psychology of Interested Adolescents." *Journal of Youth and Adolescence* 32.1 (2003): 27–35. Web.

Hunter and famed psychologist Csikszentmihalyi propose that one way to discover why so many children are disengaged is to find and research interested and happy adolescents and compare them to their peers. One of the key findings is that engaged adolescents feel more control over their lives.

- Kohn, Alfie. "Choices for Children: Why and How to Let Students Decide." *Phi Delta Kappan* 75.1 (1993): 8–16, 18–21. Web.

Controversial author Alfie Kohn writes for the *NY Times*, his own website, and nonfiction books about children and intrinsic motivation issues.

- Malone, Thomas W. "Toward a Theory of Intrinsically Motivating Instruction." *Cognitive Science* 5.4 (1981): 333–69. Web.

Thomas Malone's seminal work on the gamification of learning explores why video games are so engaging (even back in 1980!), and how education can be as well.

- Rich, Motoko. "A New Assignment: Pick Books You Like." *The New York Times*, Aug. 29, 2009. Web.

This article describes the controversy over student-selected reading in middle school grades.

- Wigfield, Allan. "Engagement and Motivation in Writing." *Handbook of Reading Research,* by John T. Guthrie. Vol. 3. Routledge: Abingdon, 2000, 403–22. Print.

Wigfield and Guthrie review the research on best practices for reading engagement.

- Williams, J. D., T. L. Wallace, and H. C. Sung. "Providing Choice in Middle Grade Classrooms: An Exploratory Study of Enactment Variability and Student Reflection." *The Journal of Early Adolescence* 36.4 (2015): 527–50. Web.

    Williams, Wallace, and Sung suggest that choice and reflection increase intrinsic motivation among middle schoolers.

What to Watch

- ExtraCreditz. "Extra Credits: Gamifying Education." YouTube, May 13, 2012. Web.

    These game developers created the Extra Credits series to explain various scientific ideas with animation and engaging voiceovers. They created multiple episodes about gamification and its effects on marketing, education, medicine, and, of course, video game design.

Chapter Five

Purpose and Relevancy

Making It Real Makes a Difference

"Why are we learning this?" Too often the answer is: It's on the test; you'll need it next year; it's the standard. While an enthusiastic and knowledgeable teacher can make that enough for students already motivated for academic success, learning is more powerful when it speaks to their personal purposes. Teaching that begins with asking about learners' goals and purposes, begins with the assumption that students have their own minds and agencies.

What Richard Ryan, Edward Deci, and Mihaly Csikszentmihalyi have described as "flow," "competency," and "internal motivations," we, as teachers, can simplify to "purpose," as does the research from applied psychology, management, and business communication. The work in intrinsic motivation for the business world, including learning that the employees who believe in the purpose of their work enjoy working more and work harder, should speak to the education community about why making education more purposeful is important.

As Adam Grant found in the University of Pennsylvania study, college development callers requesting donations for scholarship programs were more effective and happier about their work after meeting the recipients of the scholarships. Similarly, project-based learning (PBL), service learning, and genius hours have more student engagement simply because they make the learning more real.

Additionally, research by Edward Deci, Richard Ryan, and fellow researcher Christopher Niemiec suggests that college graduates with "purpose goals" are happier and less depressed than graduates with "profit goals," even those that meet their profit goals. While it may be tempting to dismiss profit in the classroom, similar research for education works if you just swap the words "profit" and "grades." Students focused on getting top grades, instead of learning to achieve their own purposes, report more anxiety and less positive feelings about school and themselves, according to Niemiec.

HOW CAN TEACHERS DESIGN ASSIGNMENTS WITH THE INTRINSIC MOTIVATION NEEDED FOR PURPOSE?

Students have their own purposes as humans, just as each writing piece has its own purpose for being written. And like a piece of writing, the work is better when its purpose is considered first.

First, instructional goals should be transparent and connected to learning goals they help make. This is *not* just putting the standard on the board. The Common Core Standards for literacy recommend teaching and working toward a broad range of writing purposes and audiences that appear in the world outside of school. Students should have an idea of how their previous skills have built to this task and how they can use their skills in possible futures.

Perhaps they learned to list facts about an animal in second grade; they learned to research and cite well in sixth grade; they learned to write for a formal audience in eighth grade; they learned to synthesize multiple sources in a single topical paragraph their sophomore year; and now they are ready to bring those elements together in the junior year in a formal report of information—a genre that can be used in various careers, from scientist to fashion buyer to state trooper.

Now they have an idea of what skills they already bring to this genre, an idea of how they might use the skill outside of the classroom, and last, an excellent mentor text to see the key features of the genre with ideas about language appropriate to purpose and audience of writing. Learning skills for a state standard can be purposeful as they work on mastery. Even without a connection to their own futures or their passions, the continuum of mastery creates its own purpose. Humans like to master new skills.

Beyond the purposeful mastery of new skills, language arts instruction lends itself to all kinds of communication and meaning making that are relevant outside of the school day. Reading and listening are one of the principal ways we take in information, and that seeking of new ideas and synthesis helps the learning of new information, leading to opportunities for writing, performing, and applying that knowledge. Simulations, hypotheticals, and PBL are all ways to make learning purposeful.

IMPLICATIONS FOR COURSE DESIGN—REAL ASSESSMENTS, CONNECTING TO THEIR REAL LIVES

Relevant curriculum makes every subject more engaging. Every subject has its specialty in making content relevant to students, but backward planning, PBL, inquiry learning, and genius hour are general ideas to make every curriculum more purposeful.

Backward planning goes back to teacher purpose: Why are you teaching what you are teaching, what are the end goals? Sharing with students the purpose of their learning gives them more buy-in, more reason to care about their learning, especially when the learning goals connect with learning they care about like future careers, interpersonal relationships, self-knowledge, and so forth.

PBL, although difficult to construct, are projects that emulate real-life learning by leading students through experiences leading to a learning goal. Inquiry learning, similar to PBL, directs students to an over-arching question that they must research and make meaning of with what they find. A key component of any large project must be learning skills before final assessments of skills; good projects are not just about creative presentation of content.

As education becomes more focused on standards and accountability, an undeniable casualty has consistently been projects and time for students to explore individual interests. Using the idea of "genius hour" to allow kids to learn about their passions is one way to bring academic coaching and rigor to student interests. Genius hour, like 20 percent time in the business world, as written about by Ryan Tate and others, allows students time to deeply explore their own interests in an academic way.

Students in high school often comment that they do not have time to read books of their own choosing anymore, and that they used to write for fun but just no longer have time. Some schools offer genius hour electives as a way to facilitate that academic coaching. Students register for and attend genius hour classes where they can follow their individual passions with an academic teacher there as a guide into the intellectual world of their choice.

The student in love with photography would use the genius hour elective to read, research, interview, and explore photography beyond their photography class, ultimately reporting their findings and being responsible for mentoring beginning photography students. Or a student interesting in starting their own horse training business would research relevant business models and steps, create marketing, and interview experts.

Other schools integrate large student-led projects into multiple courses to make room for that kind of individual inquiry, allowing students to choose their focus for science fairs, History Day projects, research papers, and presentations.

That kind of school culture change can begin in the classroom when student purpose shapes course, curriculum, and classroom decisions. There is a module in California's Expository Reading and Writing Curriculum for eighth grade that asks students to research tap and bottled water and ends with them writing a proposal to their school board making recommendations about whether tap or bottled water would be better for their school community. Students enjoy the unit because the purpose is real and affects what

> I admit that I work at a high school that does this better than most. Our recent accreditation report commented that the students move with purpose throughout their day and activities. What gives them purpose? Obviously our career and technical education courses in automotive, agriculture, culinary arts, welding, digital media, floral design, and wood shops promote relevancy, but there is not a program on campus not connected to the community doing real things. Water sampling in biology, real-world internships in agriculture business, composting and school garden in environmental science, art shows in local businesses, and community service integrated into every sport team, club, and the associated student body. The language arts department created a multi-year service learning program that will be discussed separately, but relevancy is a driving factor in the curriculum. Freshman learn about local indigenous people and history, sophomores do family history projects, and all grades learn technology and explore careers. The department assesses regularly the following:
>
> - Are we teaching skills that relate to their future lives?
> - Are the readings timely or engaging?
> - Do the assessments actually assess the intended skill?
> - Is the sequence of skills integrated, so that students make progress?
>
> The administration did not urge teachers and staff to create purposeful curriculum and programs. They did, however, hire qualified staff and trust them to follow their passions and purposes (and choose their own professional development!). The programs and school philosophy grew slowly. The principal, Clint Duey, recognized what had been created in the global education humanities curriculum for ninth and tenth graders and the way all of the programs connected out to authentic purposes in the community. He decided that was the campus focus, or, as he says, "More than any test score, any sports standings, we make good people who know how to make good out in the world."

they drink every day, but it also teaches them how to write persuasive letters to help change their communities in ways that feel real and purposeful to them while simultaneously practicing letter writing, research, and persuasive argumentation.

HOW DOES SERVICE LEARNING AFFECT STUDENT ENGAGEMENT?

Service learning taps into students' sense of contribution and purpose. It builds skills for community and life engagement and also provides motivation to come to school and stay out of trouble. Community service aids the community, but service learning allows learning goals and content to connect to student autonomy and purpose.

Often community service is imposed on students as required hours for a class or diploma, or as a punishment dispensed by a court or disciplinary system. Service learning is built into the learning and provides skill practice of academic instruction. It answers the question, why are we learning this? The best service learning calls on students to connect with their own interests and beliefs on what can be done to improve their community.

Service-learning programs are an especially easy fit in literacy instruction since real change happens only after research, written communication, and real public speaking practice. According to Maurice Elias of Rutgers University, a researcher on social and emotional learning, service learning connects students to community in a way that enriches both.

The community service hours requirement at so many schools has been morphed into service-learning programs.

I wrote a program for the high school where I teach, Change the World, that challenges every senior to connect their passions and strengths to the community and world in ways that make things better. The key component of the Change the World program is that the writing, researching, and public speaking taught in the classroom have a very relevant application to both them and their projects. The program has expanded to multiple grades now, with sophomores writing and researching problem-response papers to discover means to deal with world problems, juniors writing and researching a multi-section research paper exploring an idea, and seniors completing the project over the entire school year.

The research leads them to discover the ways their own lives have been impacted by adults volunteering and how they can use what they have learned in school to impact others. In the six years of the program, student interests have led them to researching, writing, and lobbying for changes in the city ordinance about secondhand smoke; increased programs for art, physical education, science, chess, and body image in local after-school programs; better eighth grade orientation and freshman support at our high school; city-wide celebration of National Poetry Month; a school garden and compost system; coordination with state and federal wildlife agencies to remove non-native species and protect watershed; and writing (and receiving!) energy auditing grants to encompass five different schools.

These projects were conceived and implemented by students, with classroom learning supporting the professional communication skills necessary, as well as coaching provided by school staff and community mentors to help students take on these ambitious plans. Students who have been through the program report more confidence getting jobs and running projects in the future. As newcomers to the job world, the experience students gain in the Change the World project helps them network and get job experience.

Many alumni seek out volunteering opportunities as college students and young adults: creating soccer and nutrition programs for low-income families, providing free tax services at the local library, and volunteering at local elementary schools. The communication skills they learn in the project follow them into the rest of their lives.

PERFORMANCE MAKES IT REAL

A shortcut to relevancy that we use perhaps too sparingly in education is speaking and listening. Everything feels more real to students when they get a chance to discuss in small groups or present to their peers. Students are in a time of self-discovery, finding out who they are and how others are different. Argumentation and discovering various philosophical stances invariably need to be talked through before they can write with any authority. Listening for information, inference, and tone are sophisticated skills they will use throughout their lives.

Speaking and listening are difficult to grade. It's why we shy away from them in the classroom, but there are few skills we teach that are more relevant to students' future careers and personal success. They know it. Students feel self-conscious as speakers, yet know they would benefit from more confidence and skill in speaking and listening. When students can choose their own goals, they often choose more confidence in speaking to large groups, more skills in talking to people different from themselves, and being able to really understand the people around them. So, then, how do we frame the assessing and scoring of these valuable skills?

Part of the problem is that speaking and listening are not merely academic skills but reflections of students' most basic selves. There is shame attached to not being charming and interpersonally adept in our society. How do teachers score that and not make people feel worse about their communication skills?

Divorcing assessment and scoring as students learn speaking and listening skills helps remove some of the anxiety they feel. Speaking and listening often are so fundamental to personality that they report stress and anxiety when they know they are being graded on those skills. The answer isn't to avoid speaking and listening, though, but to break them into manageable chunks. Unlike reading and writing, many teachers weren't specifically taught how to teach speaking and listening, so there can be a disconnect between what students need and teacher ability to break down those skills.

Some pundits have argued that the current generation, raised on digital devices, is disadvantaged in this area, having spent less time in face-to-face communication in comparison to previous generations. Too often speaking and listening are not explicitly taught or practiced, and then grades for speaking are determined by high-stakes, large audience, formal presentations.

This would be the equivalent of not asking kids to write until the end-of-semester research paper, and then being surprised that they don't know how to be successful at that task. Listening, on the other hand, is often not taught or

Purpose and Relevancy

Table 5.1. Speaking: Ways to Make It Real

Activity	Grade Levels Where Most Applicable			
	K–3	4–6	7–8	9–12
Speaking				
Poem recitation	X	X	X	X
Author's chair	X	X	X	
Role playing	X	X	X	X
Acting out stories/plays	X	X	X	X
Science/history fairs		X	X	X
Community presentations to school boards, city councils, and so forth			X	X

scored and the only indicator of skill is the general ability to follow instructions from the teacher.

A better way to approach speaking includes more ungraded practice, frank conferencing about current skill levels, focus on growth, practice with the fractured components of these complex skills, and explicit instruction and practice in listening for varied purposes. There's more than one way to achieve ungraded, but assessed, practice, but in some classrooms many speaking opportunities have small scores attached to doing them, no matter the skill, coupled with feedback on delivery and strategies for the next attempt.

Students know practicing and playing with different strategies will not hurt their grades, and the practice and experimentation make them more confident for larger assignments. Students also are encouraged to create their own speaking and listening goals, and they often choose, for example, better notetaking, being perceived as credible and trustworthy in interpersonal communication, leading small groups, handling conflict at work better, or presenting fearlessly. Teacher strategies based on their individual problems in individual quarterly conferences, and practice often, in and out of class, create more confident public speakers.

REAL TASKS + REAL AUDIENCES = REAL WRITERS REALLY EXCITED ABOUT LEARNING

The introduction to Common Core's English Language Arts Standards describes well-prepared students as follows: "They respond to the varying demands of audience, task, purpose, and discipline." In fact, the standards ask students as early as third grade to consider who they are writing for and to what purpose.

The difference between writing for a purpose and writing to get a grade or answer a question is obvious to reader and writer alike. But having students consider the purpose of their piece can be the first step in having them find their purpose as readers and writers, and the adults they will become. Blogs, portfolios, writing contests, letters to Santa or the city council: There are many ways to find authentic audiences for writing.

Teachers and students of all ages have found blogging to increase the purpose in writing. Knowing their work will be read by people besides their teacher changes the focus. With all students, online privacy is an issue. Students shouldn't share last names or other identifying details in their public blogs. Sites like EdModo, KidBlog, and Blogmeister create a fenced off bit of the Internet where student work is just shared with other students and family.

In later grades, students can try Blogger or WordPress, especially if they use school email addresses that filter spam and further insulate students' personal lives. Beyond the obvious safety issues, not all writing needs to be published and students should have control over how they share their world. No matter if the teacher thinks the writing is ready for publication, students, as the writers, should decide where that writing is in the process and if it should be published.

I teach a digital publishing class where students learn to write different genres of online content. A class blog publishes news stories and pieces of writing that need to be published but don't fit anywhere else. Each student in the class creates and curates a topical blog where they publish most of their assignments and sometimes host guest bloggers, including me and their classmates. Their blog topics are as varied as they are: agriculture, breads, political activism, psychology of video games, and photography skills and concepts.

They read and write on their blog topics weekly, delving deeply into their area of interest; no class of mine has more say in what they read and what they write. The writing assignments are broad enough that they can each find a way to make it work for them, with mentor texts chosen from the blogosphere for genres like annotated resource list, product review, response to news story. The biggest surprise has been how much they read and write beyond my expectations and how reluctant they are to submit work they feel needs more revision.

Like most writers I know, they have many pieces in process at any one time, their process is idiosyncratic to them, and they are willing to experiment in organization and delivery of their content to provide a better experience for their readers. Many teachers have also had positive experiences with digital storytelling tools that allow students to create online books or presentations, with plentiful and varied sources online for every grade. Depending on the digital storytelling tool, students can share their work with only the teacher, the parent, and a few select peers, with their whole class, or with the entire Internet.

Blogs and document sharing allow for writing feedback to happen beyond teacher feedback on drafts. Document sharing allows for real-time edits, and even synchronous digital writing conferences. More dynamic than red marks on a page, document sharing allows for conversations about purpose and effect, with instructors or peers. Even trained third graders can share documents with peers and give real feedback about effectiveness and details, not to mention editing. A subtle switch in digital editing of papers is to toggle from editing to suggesting. Most of us would suggest edits on an adult peer's writing, not change it for them. Student writers deserve the same autonomy on their work and benefit from doing the mental heavy lifting of making suggested edits. Real audiences make a difference.

Portfolios, in general, give students choices about how they are assessed, and keeping a portfolio makes mastery obvious and drives student learning goals. After training students to value growth more than grades, keeping collections of their work allows them to set their own goals and monitor their own progress. When students see their reading and writing practice as purposeful work toward their goals, their engagement in writing improves.

Other ways to consider making writing more real include writing to newspapers, politicians, parents, essays for scholarships, or writing contests. Anytime students are writing to someone besides the teacher, their writing is more focused, more real. Many teachers actually urge students to picture someone they know when writing. They explain ideas further, the argument is more persuasive, and they conclude their work, not merely ending it.

Table 5.2. Writing: Ways to Make It Real

Activity	Grade Levels Where Most Applicable			
	K–3	4–6	7–8	9–12
Writing				
Stories to illustrate	X	X	X	
Lists: grocery, favorite things, books they want to read, and goals	X	X	X	X
Writing for their understanding of difficult stuff: math, world events, different religious ideas, what makes an animal a mammal, and political systems	X	X	X	X
Conference letters about their learning to parents and teachers	X	X	X	X
Persuasive letters to instigate change	X	X	X	X
Poetry to perform	X	X	X	X
Reflective narratives about why they love their family for holiday gifts	X	X	X	X
Writing contests: stories, essays, and poetry	X	X	X	X

Table 5.3. Reading: Ways to Make It Real

Activity	Grade Levels Where Most Applicable			
	K–3	4–6	7–8	9–12
Reading				
Read chosen book for pleasure	X	X	X	X
Read to partners for understanding	X	X		
Read to parents	X	X		
Read for individually chosen research report, for example, habitats, mammals, and states		X	X	X
Read aloud to younger students		X	X	X
Read ingredients in favorite foods		X	X	X
Read to connect topic to their lives	X	X	X	X
Read to think about future careers	X	X	X	X

READING: A PORTAL TO A WORLD OF YOUR MAKING

Primary-age kids love to visit the school library and choose their own books. When the librarian or aide asks why that book this week, they don't hesitate: "This girl looks like the kind of friend I want to be"; "I'm going to be an astronaut too"; or "I like the words in this book and want to learn what they mean." They have learning goals, and they know reading is one way to reach those goals.

As academic expectations grow beyond enjoying reading and gaining reading skills, so much of the reading assigned is about teacher purpose instead of their own. Despite the societal stereotype, students read more words per day than they did a generation ago, much of it digital. They seek out and find reading about their interests, celebrities, video game cheat sheets, future careers, make-up tutorials, and fitness tips. Students welcome reading choice and value research and writing opportunities that allow them to read purposefully in their interests like research papers or blogging.

Assignments like these allow students to fall deep into their chosen rabbit hole, like the student who recently started writing about psychology use in video games and ended up deciphering psychology journal articles on reward schedules. Students are also more motivated to read and more motivated to read difficult texts when the text's goals align with their own purpose.

TEACHER PURPOSE KEY TO PASSIONATE CLASSROOMS

Kids' needs in the classrooms are as varied as they are. Thankfully, teachers do not have the same life experience, education, beliefs, or strengths as the instructors down the hall. Our individual strengths, all 3.5 million teachers in the United States, give us different purposes. While teachers do not work for the high pay and respect, every teacher brings their own purpose and passion to the classroom. If you're not sure of yours, consider what you want your students to remember about how you made them feel when they look back as adults.

> I recently had a former student send me a card thanking me for how she felt empowered to begin her adult life by what she learned in my class, meaning she knew how to steer her brain and how to adult and, therefore, knew how to find her success. That's what I want for every one of my students. My purpose—that is, my passion for positive psychology and metacognition and language theory, my strengths in helping developing others, and my belief in community service—makes me a more passionate teacher. David Burgess, in his book *Teach Like a Pirate*, urges teachers to connect their subject passion, their teaching passion, and their interests from their personal life to help give their classrooms their unique purpose.

Purposeful, passionate teachers, no matter what part of teaching gives them that passion, make better teachers. Students often lack enthusiasm for the nuts and bolts of what we teach, and it's our job to lend them ours! Pundits may suggest new teachers are better at inspiring kids, but the problem may be simply that experienced teachers may forget that their purpose in teaching is their most important resource and let that energy be tapped by all of the positions of leadership they're asked to take on as people with more organizational knowledge.

In the world of standardized teaching scripts, teachers varying their curriculum based on their own passions and strengths may seem anathema. Yet asking me to teach preschool, or carpentry, or accounting would be a waste of my strengths and enthusiasm. The same is true of the teachers in the school near you; our purposes are the muscle we bring to teaching.

TEACHERS AND WRITERS TALK

Service learning taps into students' sense of contribution and purpose. It builds skills for community and life engagement and also provides motivation to come to school and stay out of trouble. Teachers must spend a bit more time to establishing the rationale for assignments, and generating some sense of relevance or buy-in from students in order to engage intrinsic motivation. But at times, there are some assignments we all do because we have to, for credit or to avoid undesired consequences.

—*Maurice J. Elias*

About Maurice: Maurice J. Elias, Ph.D., teaches, lectures, researches, and writes about social-emotional learning from the psychology department of Rutgers University.

Take-away: Dr. Elias proposes that service learning and other methods of increasing purpose engage students, keeping them coming to school and doing the less-than-motivating tasks necessary in our educational systems.

> *Electronic publishing can help students develop purposeful writing in a quite a few ways. First and foremost, it provides them with an authentic audience. All students hit that certain point in their writing where they write for an audience of one-of their teachers. I would have to say that students, for the most part, have figured out what a certain teacher expects, and writes to that expectation. By doing that they lose their voice. Writing and publishing electronically opens them up, makes them vulnerable, and because that is pretty uncomfortable, they need to find their voice.*
>
> *It also allows them to represent their thoughts, feelings, and attitudes to the larger world. They have to learn how to express themselves in ways that can be understood.*
>
> *When publishing online students need to connect to their writerly selves to tell their story, but they also need to be ready, mentally, for the reaction of others. This is where mindset comes in to play. Students who publish electronically need to be ready to understand that not everyone will appreciate or like what they write. IN fact, some people will work hard to tear it down. By having a growth mindset and the skills needed to take the bad with the good, students will become more comfortable in their purpose as writers.*
>
> *The biggest thing I can stress is allowing students to decide the level of "publicness" when they are publishing digitally. As educators, we need to give gentle pushes for greatness, but if a student is not ready to share it will totally backfire.*
>
> —Carrie Ann Gehringer

About Carrie: Carrie Ann Gehringer teaches middle school language arts and coaches volleyball in South Dakota.

Take-away: Many teachers, like Gehringer, use blogs in increasingly academic and innovative ways. Resources like EdCamps, Computer Using Educators (CUE), Google for Education, and others help teachers connect with other teachers to find best practices and best products to support student writing online.

> *Authentic audiences! As an English teacher focused on global competencies as well as writing and speaking, I find that when students have an audience and purpose that is real, they are more intrinsically motivated and I don't have to do as much work to motivate them. Essay competitions, our cross-cultural blog with students in Morocco, school-wide poetry slams, and projects presented to*

the entire community tend to motivate them more than an assignment for which I am their only audience.

—*Tara Nuth Kajtaniak*

About Tara: Tara Nuth Kajtaniak, an alumni of the U.S. State Department's Teachers for Global Classrooms program, a member of the Institute for Teaching's East Bay Think Tank, Global Learning EdWeek Blog contributor, and presenter of cultural complexity/sensitivity workshops, teaches high school English and champions global education. Connect with her on Twitter @TaraNuth or via her blog, GlobalEducationGuide.org.

Take-away: Connecting their communication out to the greater world, whether it be another continent or another city, gives purpose to their writing and reading. The world is bigger than students often realize. When teachers have students write stories, blogs, or letters to real people across the world, students are challenged to show who they are and what they value through their writing.

In my research with State Teachers of the Year, I've found that professional growth is not only integral to overall motivation, morale, and job satisfaction, but relevant, well-designed professional development experiences are desired for optimal professional growth. The variables that teachers associate with effective professional growth include opportunities for collaboration, self-reflection, and prospects for movement along a viable career continuum.

Unfortunately, as most teachers would agree, many traditional professional development practices are irrelevant, inconsistent, and unsustainable. As such, many teachers take the initiative to pursue professional growth opportunities on their own, and they are usually driven by a sense of obligation to improve for the sake of their students and the profession as a whole.

In general, it seems that what makes professional growth meaningful and valuable are the basic human needs as prescribed by Self-Determination Theory: autonomy, competence, and relatedness. These needs nicely parallel the precepts of Dweck's growth mindset. For teachers, as with anyone, motivation and morale are sustained with enhanced self-efficacy, validation, and growth. Meaningful professional growth endeavors are an important variable in this process.

—*David Bosso*

About David: David Bosso, Connecticut teacher of the year and researcher on public school teachers, writes about teachers and motivation.

Take-away: Bosso reminds teachers that autonomy, competence, relatedness are as important for teachers as they are for students and should start with educators in order to make long-term changes in classrooms.

LEARN MORE

What to Read

- Bosso, David. "Guest Blog: This Is What I Am." *Center for Teaching Quality*. Mar. 18, 2014. Web.
  Bosso explores how teacher purpose connects to student learning.
- Burgess, Dave. *Teach Like a Pirate: Increase Student Engagement, Boost Your Creativity, and Transform Your Life as an Educator*. San Diego, CA: Dave Burgess Consulting, 2012. Print.
  Dave Burgess argues in this book that finding a way to be enthusiastic about the curriculum should be teacher's first priority, since their passion is the wave that students ride into the material and teachers must find the purpose in what they teach before they can adequately share it with students.
- Christensen, Linda. *Reading, Writing, and Rising Up: Teaching about Social Justice and the Power of the Written Word*. Milwaukee, WI: Rethinking Schools, 2000. Print.
  In this work, and also her work *Teaching for Joy and Justice*, Christensen explains how reading and writing can empower students by creating activism.
- Elias, Maurice J. "How to Bring Service Learning to Your School." *Edutopia*. June 17, 2009. Web.
  Dr. Elias' work from Rutgers University in Social Emotional Learning influences this article that argues service learning increases engagement, academic outcomes, and career readiness.
- Ferriter, Bill. "CTQ." *Blogging Resources for Classroom Teachers*. Sept. 2, 2013. Web.
  This Center for Teaching Quality article is a good entry into blogging with students.
- Gagne, Marylene, and Edward L. Deci. "Self-determination Theory and Work Motivation." Published online in *Wiley InterScience* (www.interscience.wiley.com). DOI: 10.1002/job.322. *Journal of Organizational Behavior* 26.4 (2005): 331–62. Web.
  This pivotal article explains the history of intrinsic motivation research for work and adds the newer research that aligns with personal beliefs and goals, purpose, increased employee performance and satisfaction.
- Hamon, Keith. "Teaching Writing with Google Docs." *Fractus Learning*. Apr. 30, 2014. Web. Oct. 28, 2016.
  This *Fractus Learning* article describes best practices in GoogleDoc editing to make revision more purposeful.

- Jackson, Lorrie. "How to Blog With Young Students." *Education World*. Feb. 8, 2012. Web.
  This article explains details of blogging with young students.
- McCarthy, John. "4 Paths to Engaging Authentic Purpose and Audience." *Edutopia*. Apr. 13, 2015. Web.
  This article connects student purpose to real audiences.
- Smith, Anna. "A Thousand Writers: Voices of the NWP." *English Journal* 104.3 (2015): 81–84. National Council of the Teachers of English, Jan. 2015. Web.
  This first-person narrative reminds teachers of the personal purpose of student writing.
- Smith, Emily Esfahani. "There's More to Life Than Being Happy." *The Atlantic*. Jan. 9, 2013. Web.
  This *Atlantic* article highlights the value of purpose in creating a meaningful life.
- Tate, Ryan. *The 20% Doctrine: How Tinkering, Goofing Off, and Breaking the Rules at Work Drive Success in Business*. New York, NY: Harper Business, 2012. Kindle.
  This book illustrates with business case studies how employers can nurture employee purpose for substantial innovation.
- Tovani, Cris. "The Power of Purposeful Reading." *Educational Leadership* issue Oct. 2005, Reading Comprehension. *ASCD* 63.2 (2005): 48–51. Web.
  In this article, Tovani explains how to guide teens to read with purpose.

What to Watch

- Deci, Edward, and Stephanie Dandeneau. "Professor Edward Deci on Self-Determination Theory." *Vimeo*. Feb. 26, 2012. Web.
  Edward Deci of the University of Rochester explains how the theory of self-determination predicts happiness from purposeful and engaging behaviors.

Chapter Six

Fostering Connection and Positivity

Reading, writing, and speaking are all social endeavors that connect us to each other. Writers don't write alone and readers don't read alone, and intrinsic motivation research tells us that connection and working toward a common goal can motivate people to work harder and smarter. Teachers know that the culture of their classroom and school affect how safe students feel physically, but also how safe they feel taking risks or thinking new thoughts. Learning and engagement happen when students feel emotionally safe and cognitively challenged.

CREATING A SAFE SPACE TO BROADEN AND BUILD

Psychologist Barbara Fredrickson in her books *Positivity* and *Love 2.0* argues that positive emotions that psychologists were so slow to study are as necessary to our survival as fear and anger. It's been long understood that fear and anger can make us act in self-protective ways: outrun competitors, stand up for ourselves, and obtain a boost of energy to fight.

Barbara Fredrickson and other psychologists decided to study the value of positive emotions. They found that positive emotions cause people to connect, learn, grow emotionally, and even heal. Cognitively, positive emotions allow for more creativity, persistence in difficult tasks, and deeper recall. In short, students must have positive feelings about the classroom and themselves to do their best learning. Teachers and schools have tried to create good feelings about school for children for decades.

The newer research on positive psychology and experience suggests that positive emotions can't be manufactured, that the hedonism of flashy videos and pizza for lunch bring as much long-term emotional sustenance as diet soda brings to our bodies. Positive emotions can change the school experience when they are eudaimonistic, creating emotional and cognitive connections between the students and the lives they want to live. Learning and literacy can be paths to these connections. Eudaimonism describes the life satisfaction based on purpose, mastery, and connection.

OTHER WAYS TO POSITIVITY BESIDES COMPLIMENTING

Although esteem building and complimenting students to protect their self-esteem were big ideas decades ago, empty praise may stroke egos in the short term but have unnecessary long-term effects. As education writer Alfie Kohn commented in an *Education World* interview in 2000:

> There's a place for unconditional love and support and attention and encouragement. That's what kids need. There's also a place for feedback: providing kids with information about their accomplishments—when they need it. But praise is different from either of these things. First, it's conditional: It says I'll give you attention and support only when you please me, when you meet my standards, when you jump through my hoops. Second, it's not feedback; it's judgment. And kids don't need, or thrive on, constant judgment, even if it's in the form of "Good job!" That tends to create praise junkies, who quickly grow to be dependent on someone else to evaluate what they've done.

Kohn argues that praise can function as an extrinsic reward when there's too much of it, when it's insincere, and when it functions as currency, and, like extrinsic rewards, praise can replace the desire to do an action because you enjoy it, making it only a short-term means to an end.

Positive regard and observation without praise make kids feel noticed and appreciated without trafficking in praise. Imagine a classroom where a teacher tries to control students with praise. Everyone who fits their measure of success, perhaps beautifully structured academic support or understanding of a certain genre, receives lavish praise, but other students are never praised. The teacher might be trying to reward and support specific academic skills, but the result is a classroom where the students think that the teacher plays favorites and therefore do not trust enough to be their true selves, even the praise receivers.

Emotional principles of positive psychology are better used to make classrooms safe places to have all emotions, and places where most of the emotions are positive. A school counselor has a Post-it on her computer facing her, but usually unreadable to students across the desk. The Post-it read "Relentless Positive Regard." When asked, she explains that it is her goal for

Table 6.1. Connection versus Praise

Praise sounds like ...	Because ...	But connection and observation can sound like ...	In order to ...
Good job!	Teachers want to encourage students.	I can see how you revised to make that evidence stronger.	Show them their efforts are noticeable.
Atta boy!	Teachers want students to have positive emotions about their efforts.	I appreciate what you did there.	Make real emotional connection by acknowledging our real emotions.
You did great!	Teachers want students to keep trying.	A smile	Make necessary feedback count more, sometimes teachers just need to be quiet more.

working with every student: liking them and giving them room to be honest and hold themselves accountable.

The concept, originating with psychologist Carl Rogers, is widely used in social work, especially in prisons where being treated with respect happens so rarely. Enjoy your students. Mark Muraven and other researchers of willpower have found that emotional stress and lack of autonomy use up the stores of willpower, the ability to persevere. Put another way, students need you to like them in order to do their best learning.

RESEARCH SUGGESTS THAT SOCIAL CONNECTION MOTIVATES MORE THAN REWARDS

Humans are social creatures. As a teacher, you have probably experienced in your classroom a time when students felt more trepidation (or excitement!) about speaking or reading their writing in front of their peers than they felt about their grade or wanting a reward.

Communication is, by its very nature, social, and teachers can leverage the social components of literacy to make the learning more relevant, but also we can use the social web of connections in our classrooms to inspire students to become their best selves. According to researchers Lili Tian, Huan Chen, and E. Scott Huebner, not only does relatedness affect student motivation more than short-term, tangible rewards, but of all the components of self-determination theory (relatedness, competency, and autonomy), relatedness has the highest correlation with school satisfaction and performance for adolescents.

Social support and emotional safety at school matters more for teen happiness at school than choosing what book to read or seeing growth in chemistry or Spanish. For children of all ages, competency is the most important motivator, but adolescents especially are motivated by learning environments where they feel they belong. If that belonging doesn't happen in the classroom, students will seek relatedness in outside cultures that may or may not value literacy. Classroom cultures can help even struggling students see and honor their progress, making them feel more competent, and can build social habits that build people and relationships.

AT THE SCHOOL LEVEL

School culture expert Raven Coit not only teaches English, but she takes her activities director knowledge and experience to conferences and public events to discuss how to change school culture by reshaping school habits. She explains how she sets up her students to create patterns of culture:

> We begin each year with a discussion of our vision and values. Over the summer, we create a list of values we believe are crucial to who we are as Huskies. We then develop a vision for what our school would look like this school year if we lived by those values. When we plan each activity—each rally, dance, welcome day, kindness week—we ask ourselves how this activity is living our values. After each activity, we check in again: how effectively did we cultivate our values of kindness and empathy during this week? How do we know when it's working? In this way, we stay focused on the bigger purpose of creating a culture of care on our campus, instead of the distracting details of water bottles, Easter eggs, and poster painting.

She argues that while students might choose to do leadership activities out of a sense of importance, when encouraged to act out their values, they are connected to other students and their purpose. This intentional, value-led creation of school culture can lead to transformation of toxic habits like booing at new freshmen at rallies:

> Through subtle shifts, we changed that tradition in just three years. Link Crew leaders rushed out of their comfort zones in the junior and senior class sections at rallies and ran to help the freshmen cheer when they were introduced. When we empowered 15% of the upper two classes to use their leadership to create a positive, welcoming legacy, the rest of the older students followed their example. And by ending the cycle of booing and negativity, the younger classes lost

the urge to get revenge for their own negative experiences. Instead, they did what was done to them—they cheered and welcomed our newest huskies! It took just one year to significantly shift a crucial early experience at our school. Then it took just two more years before no one remembered a time when freshmen were booed! Our current students cheer for our new students because they learned from our leaders—huskies are welcoming and kind. That's just who we are.

Maurice Elias from Rutgers University argues that social emotional learning, teaching kids how to connect, is the most important teaching for students, improving school and life satisfaction as well as cognitive performance.

AT THE CLASSROOM LEVEL

Teachers are responsible for the culture in their classrooms. Between busses, school shootings, bullying, and earthquake drills, schools take student safety seriously. And with all of the threats to students, it may feel like it's too much to make our classrooms emotionally safe places, but the purpose of school is learning and helping students find their place in the world.

Classrooms where it is emotionally safe, where they can be themselves and experiment with forms of communication and expression, will probably be more important than learning to wear closed-toe sandals on the bus for school safety and success.

The organization Partnership for 21st Century Learning, a coalition of the U.S. Department of Education and businesses like Apple, Microsoft, and Time Warner, argues that collaboration and communication are pivotal for student and employee success in the modern world. Direct instruction in collaboration and interpersonal communication is necessary for students to learn to interact professionally toward a common goal.

Project-based learning, inquiry learning, service learning, career education, mentor programs, book clubs, literature circles, writers' workshop, process-oriented guided inquiry learning (POGIL)—no matter how teachers accomplish it, students need to communicate with each other and their community to create emotional connections and positive communication experiences.

CONNECTING OUT

Connecting out to the community and world doesn't only infuse learning with more purpose, it provides emotional connection and connection with people outside the school. The more adults a child trusts, the better off the child is at resisting mental illness and getting help when they need it, according to the American Psychological Association. Direct instruction in holding conversations with adults, shaking hands, professional email, and body language makes kids more comfortable collaborating with adults, and all of those skills should be practiced in the classroom on each other.

The Common Core speaking and listening standards invite us to teach students to talk to each other, working toward a purposeful goal. As early as sixth grade, the standards call on students to set goals for conversations, be collegial in tone, and be able to build on each other's ideas in conversation. Those academic standards that are also requirements for success in the workforce can make students happier and more confident as those skills translate into more emotional connections with the people around them.

Educators, especially in middle and high school, might not believe that they are teaching social skills, but the listening and speaking skills listed in the Common Core literacy standards translate into the conversation and communication skills they will use in their homes with their loved ones and friends. Listening and speaking, paired with effective collaboration, and knowledge of personality dynamics make students better prepared for social, as well as academic, success, according to studies from Maryland.

IT'S MORE THAN GROUP WORK

Group work has become so ubiquitous in American schools that teachers and students forget why it's important and the key components of its success. Teachers shouldn't assign group work just because it helps make learning more fun, integrates students of different academic skills, or makes for fewer final products to grade.

Group work, or cooperative learning, allows for practice of social skills; if structured correctly, encourages the collaboration in the 21st Century Framework; and makes students more engaged in and better able to remember their learning, according to researchers Caruso and Wooley as reported by NYU Arts & Science. Effective group work includes a way to score the collaboration as well as the output and values all of the skills necessary to work as a group, including listening, speaking, social skills, notetaking. There are ways to incorporate collaborative learning in all kinds of subjects, ages, and classrooms, including digital.

All of the methods in the cooperative learning chart invite students to create meaning together, negotiating with each other for richer understanding and longer-lasting learning.

Table 6.2. Cooperative Learning Types

	Inquiry-based	Literature-based	Writing-based
Primary	Project-based learning (PBL), Montessori method	Read-aloud, read-to-friend	Writer's chair, writing conference, group stories
Elementary	PBL	Book centers, book clubs	Writer's chair, writing conference, group stories
Middle school	POGIL, PBL	Literature circles, Book clubs	Writing conference, revision buddies
High school	POGIL, PBL	Literature circles, book club, Socratic seminar	Writing conference, Praise, Question, Wish peer review

Project-based learning (PBL) requires students to take on real projects that require learning along the way, instead of as an assessment or product at the end of learning.

Process-oriented guided inquiry learning (POGIL) is a more structured method of PBL that can be tailored to specific content standards. "The process allows them to construct new understandings while they simultaneously develop key process skills, including critical thinking, problem solving, and collaboration," writes Laura Trout in *POGIL Activities for High School Biology*.

Read-aloud and read-to-a-friend are techniques used in early grades to have kids use each other to discover new vocabulary and content when students have often heard words they have never read before and need to hear the words aloud to guess at meaning. Together students can read at higher levels than alone.

Writer's chair is a variation of read-aloud, but for writing, where students read their writing to the group while sitting in the writer's chair. It's a way of sharing writing and emphasizing its social nature.

Encouraging Student-centered Book Clubs

Book clubs, book groups, and literature circles all have students reading individually but coming together in group conversation and writing to further explore the bigger ideas in the book and to make connections with other. Usually literature circles have set roles for each participant, explicitly teaching collaboration parts. All work well with clear expectations of group performance and ultimate outcomes of the meetings.

Students should have a challenging learning goal to work toward to make collaborative learning about reading worthwhile. This is best used with complex texts that contain multiple perspectives or philosophies.

Growing Peer Praise in Writers' Workshop and Peer Review

Peer review builds connection and writers. Students often don't see themselves as sufficient experts in writing to give appropriate feedback, and without appropriate teacher guidelines, they can be right! Structured review like Praise, Question, Wish from the National Writing Project, checklists for mechanics and easily recognizable features like evidence or main ideas, or just being asked to quote a sentence they enjoyed and explain why it was effective all prepare beginning writers for more and more autonomy over peer review.

Ultimately, the goal is for them to seek peer review even when it's not required, to search out readers in order to always be working on improving their writing. The structured feedback allows them to see the value in receiving peer review and learn to do the revision notes with more confidence.

Early writers may only be able to give editing notes. For example, primary students may use a checklist to check for capital letters at the beginning of sentences, periods at the end of sentences, and a verb in every sentence. Slightly older students can highlight topic sentences for paragraphs, checking that each paragraph has a sentence that introduces the main point. Students can also gauge the overall effectiveness of writing in grades K–5, but they should be learning that skill on sample writings, not the writings of their peers.

Modeling specific, not general, positive and constructive feedback helps students get beyond "I really like it! It was good," so that middle and high school students can use writers' workshops or hold writing conferences in pairs or with the teacher to give specific feedback on arguments, organization, and rhetorical strategies.

STRENGTH-BASED TEAMWORK: NOT EVERYONE IS THE SAME AND THAT MAKES EVERYONE STRONGER

When Martin Seligman created the VIA Institute with Dr. Chris Peterson and Dr. Neal Mayerson, the goal was to create a survey and framework of traits linked to positive psychology and the research on all of the ways to be an effective human. Society, and our classrooms, work better when everyone brings different approaches to communication and problem-solving, and when we learn to flex those differences in a way that maximizes group potential and satisfaction.

Instead of offering students one way to work together, acknowledging their strengths gives them individual options and strategies. The idea of strength-based research and education best practices goes back to the basic idea that remediation isn't effective when learners only work on that with which they struggle. Strengths must be acknowledged and grown to come at deficits at a new angle.

Consider your friend group. Are you all equally good at party planning, offering an empathetic ear, pitching in at fence building, making jokes, or mollifying angry issues? Probably not. As social creatures, humans acknowledge our differences and create functional groups from different kinds of people. Students learn to do that at school as well, and those skills can be explicitly taught in the classroom. The VIA Institute Youth Survey of Strengths can function as a starting point for students to talk about personalities and group dynamics.

Modeling Working Together as Teacher Leaders

As much as teachers may urge students to learn each other's strengths, assume that everyone means well and is doing their best, and prompt them to communicate and talk out issues with a project, teachers seem to struggle trusting each other. Used to directing their own classrooms, it can be difficult for teachers to understand and respect others' ways of doing things. Or perhaps, like police officers, teachers have heard one too many horror stories from kids of adults behaving badly to trust the other professionals in their school or district.

Students, unfortunately, absorb not only the instruction but also the message of the behavior toward other teachers. Criticizing each other, closing our doors to cooperation, and even unequal work in collaboration are all noticed by students and become the implicit curriculum.

Of course, there are places that do school staff support and collaboration well. Key components seem to be: (1) administration encouraging communication and projects between staff members and department, (2) a school culture that encourages failure with the idea of "how can we get better if we don't experiment?" (3) administration and staff that welcome staff observing each other, and (4) an acknowledgment that all school staff, janitors to superintendents, are part of a team working toward what's best for students.

Examples of these ideas can be seen in all-school staff social functions like back-to-school barbecues before school, achievement awards for all staff presented in a public way, recognition of the work all staff does with students, and staff evaluations that suggest ways to improve without being punitive. While teachers and staff may not have a way to make these changes happen without the support of administration, some teachers have set up book groups, support networks, and observation times using preps as ways to communicate, learn from each other, and provide support.

Just like with our students, creating a school culture among staff, learning how to effectively praise and give criticism, coaching social skills, and learning to understand and utilize each other's strengths make stronger schools and ultimately, stronger students.

TEACHERS AND WRITERS TALK

Ideally teachers work as a team and model their care and respect for each other in front of our students. Our students learn how to be professionals by watching us—the professionals with whom they spend the most time in their young lives. That's why it is crucial for our school leadership to cultivate a team of teachers and staff who deeply trust each other, appreciate each other's strengths, and care for each other's successes. How to do that? To begin, we need to assume the best intent. To do that? We must see each other work. We need a regular system of observing and co-teaching to appreciate and understand the broader picture of what our colleagues do. A structured opportunity to share our successes is a great way to start. The way we do this is by sharing our "wins" to kick off each month's staff meeting. We can extend our connections by celebrating those wins and the specific people responsible for each success. Next, we need to enjoy each other. We need structured and unstructured social occasions to talk shop and talk life, too. I need to know what a great quilter my colleague in the special ed department is, and how many miles my science teacher friend bikes each day so that if my day is ruined by a double booking of the computer lab, I remember those teachers are people and friends, and I assume they have the best intent, and I don't hold a grudge. Other benefits include a more optimistic attitude at meetings, an enthusiasm for opportunities to see each other and work together, and a tendency to brag about our colleagues and all the programs on our campus serving our students.

—Raven Coit

How Do You Make Your Students Feels Safe?

It's not fancy. I tell my students directly that I will do everything in my power to make this a safe place for each of them to be who they are. I expect them to do the same. And then the hard part: I am committed to enforcing that. The first priority all the time is that we're being kind and supportive to each other. When a student is undermining the safety of the room, I ask them to step outside. We stop the class, stop the learning, and address it right away in most cases. I want students to believe me when I say it's my first priority. We get back on track right away to refocus on learning and keep the kid who messed up out of the spotlight. We don't want to embarrass them and increase the stress in the situation. Then I step outside when I can, and I ask the student, "What do you need? You seem upset or something. You're being unkind and that's not like you. So what do you need?" In this way, I communicate my support and belief in my student, even when they mess up. I am sending the message that I assume the best intent.

I believe my students would never intentionally hurt someone, so they must need some help in understanding the way they affect others.

—Raven Coit

About Raven: Raven Coit teaches in Humboldt County and writes and presents on the West Coast and Colorado about intentional school culture.

Take-away: Teachers have an opportunity to model social and emotional learning through student activities, classroom interactions, and professional collaboration with each other.

POGIL lessons begin with a question that students will be able to answer through the inquiry process at the end of the lesson. For example, here is the question written for the "Transport in Cells" lesson: How do water molecules move in and out of cells? The question "Why?" is written below the title and question. There is a paragraph of basic information and questions that set the stage for the learning process that students will undertake. The purpose of the learning is made clear at the outset of the lesson.

Students work cooperatively in self-managed teams. The team members have roles that enable the team to function more effectively. We use the same team roles as CPM (college preparatory math): task manager, facilitator, resource manager, and recorder/reporter to foster consistency among disciplines. Team members are responsible for getting the team started, asking questions, ensuring that all resources are available, and sharing the information with the entire class. Student teams work through a series of questions that includes analysis of diagrams, data tables, and illustrations (models) of scientific processes. Students collaborate, using resources such as the Internet, to answer the initial "why?" question. Inquiry learning is applicable in all grades and subjects. It allows students to become the masters of their own learning and has been shown to be superior to traditional lecture/notes style teaching in fostering retention and increasing student understanding of material. "Inquiry is the active pursuit of meaning involving thought processes that change experience to bits of knowledge" (Suchman, 1968). Recent brain studies indicate that this type of active learning actually strengthens connections in the brain and makes it more likely that material will be retained and available for applications beyond the initial learning period.

—Pam Halstead

About Pam: Nationally Board Certified Teacher and instructional coach Pam Halstead teaches biology and environmental science in Humboldt County, using cooperative literacy learning practices to encourage further reading and critical thinking.

Take-away: Cooperative inquiry learning provides a way for students to talk through and explain their learning that is suggested in the speaking and listening standards while also strengthening their understanding of the material and connection to each other.

LEARN MORE

What to Read

- Bafile, Cara. "Wire Side Chats: Carrots or Sticks? Alfie Kohn on Rewards and Punishment." *Education World*. Nov. 22, 2000.
  This interview with Alfie Kohn warns against the overuse of praise.
- Boyte, Phil. *School Culture by Design*. Raleigh, NC: Learning for Living, 2015. Print.
  Phil Boyte created Link Crew and the WEB Program, peer-mentoring programs designed to prevent student disengagement and change school culture. In this small but powerful book, Boyte discusses practical ways to affect school culture.
- Brown, Brené. *Daring Greatly: How the Courage to Be Vulnerable Transforms the Way We Live, Love, Parent, and Lead*. New York, NY: Gotham, 2012. Print.
  Dr. Brown studies shame, worthiness, and wholeheartedness at the University of Houston and has written best-selling books, including *The Gifts of Imperfection* and *Rising Strong*. In *Daring Greatly*'s chapters 5 and 6, she takes on the disengagement affecting public schools and ways to combat it.
- Coit, Raven. "Student Leaders Shape School Culture." *Edutopia*. July 21, 2016. Web. July 27, 2016. http://www.edutopia.org/discussion/student-leaders-shape-school-culture.
  Coit uses student activities to create traditions and habits that transmit school culture.
- "Collaboration and Group Work." NYU Arts & Science, 2016. Web. https://wp.nyu.edu/fas-edtech/examples/collaboration-group-work/.
  This extensive website offers examples, tools, digital collaboration tools, and scholarship about the benefits of collaborative learning.
- Durman, Tyler. *Counterintuitive: What 4 Million Teenagers Wish We Knew*. Laguna Beach, CA: Tyler Durman, 2015. Print.
  Well known as an inspirational speaker for teens, parents, and teachers, Durman's new book offers conversational and moving advice for parents and teachers about adolescent psychology.
- "Educators: Make an Impact on Your Students." *Character Strengths Reports Help Teachers Motivate Students*. VIA Institute on Character, 2016. Web. Aug. 10, 2016. http://www.viacharacter.org/www/Professionals/Character-Development.

Dr. Neal Mayerson, Dr. Martin Seligman, and Dr. Chris Peterson helped create the handbook *Character Strengths and Virtues* and VIA survey of strengths that can be used to discuss speaking, listening, and connecting styles with students. The strength-based approach acknowledges that every student has a best, and different, way to work with and influence groups.

- Elias, Maurice J. *Promoting Social and Emotional Learning: Guidelines for Educators*. Alexandria, VA: Association for Supervision and Curriculum Development, 1997. Print.

    Dr. Elias of Rutgers University, with researchers across the country, offers research and case studies about social and emotional learning.

- "Framework for 21st Century Learning—P21." Washington, DC: P21. Web. July 29, 2016. http://www.p21.org/.

    The Partnership for 21st Century Learning (P21) teams business leaders with educational leaders to push for skills that translate into workplace and societal success. They argue that social skills, interpersonal communication, and collaboration are more important in the business world than ever.

- Fredrickson, Barbara. *Positivity*. New York, NY: Crown, 2009. Print.

    Fredrickson, also the author of *Love 2.0* and many academic articles, studies the long-term physical, cognitive, and emotional effects of experiencing positive emotions. Her broaden-and-build theories explain that positive emotions, in contrast to the narrowing of choices in response to negative emotions, nurture creativity and analysis.

- Hallowell, Edward M. *The Childhood Roots of Adult Happiness: Five Steps to Help Kids Create and Sustain Lifelong Joy*. New York, NY: Ballantine, 2002. Print.

    Hallowell, a Boston psychiatrist, has written many books about busyness, ADHD, and parenting. This book breaks down research into five simplified parenting ideas.

- Kris, Deborah Farmer. "The Benefits of Helping Preschoolers Understand and Discuss Their Emotions." *MindShift*. San Francisco, CA: KQED. Apr. 13, 2015. Web. July 2, 2016. https://ww2.kqed.org/mindshift/2015/04/13/the-benefits-of-helping-preschoolers-understand-and-discuss-their-emotions/.

    This article explains the long-term benefits of naming emotions and reading fiction to small children.

- Lili Tian, Jie Zhao, and E. Scott Huebner. "School-Related Social Support and Subjective Well-Being in School among Adolescents: The Role of Self-System Factors." *Journal of Adolescence* 45 (2015): 138–48.

    This academic article discusses motivation in teenagers for attending and engaging in school.

- Muraven, Mark, Marylene Gagne, and Heather Rosman. "Helpful Self-Control: Autonomy Support, Vitality, and Depletion." *Journal of Experimental Social Psychology* 44 (2008): 573–85. Web.

    Muraven's research finds that loss of autonomy and particularly autonomy loss paired with lack of emotional connection decreases the amount of willpower people have to work from in situations requiring self-discipline.
- Seligman, Martin E. P. *Authentic Happiness: Using the New Positive Psychology to Realize Your Potential for Lasting Fulfillment*. New York, NY: Free, 2002. Print.

    Seligman, the psychologist, writer, and researcher, used his position as the president of the American Psychological Association to champion positive psychology. His books *Learned Optimism*, *The Optimistic Child*, *Authentic Happiness*, and *Flourish* explain current positive psychologist research to the layman.

What to Watch

- Tryanski, Bob. "Let X=Student Activities!" *Vimeo*. Alliance for School Activities, 2012. Web. July 1, 2016. https://vimeo.com/37342407.

    This video from Alliance for School Activities argues that activities are needed for a school culture that engages students.

Chapter Seven

Metacognition
Bringing It All Together

The most important tool educators can give students is the ability to drive their own learning, even after they leave the classroom. Metacognition, thinking about learning, is the difference between reading a chapter while not retaining any information and listening to your thought processes while using your best and tested reading strategies to understand and apply your chapter's reading. Metacognition means knowing your best times to write or study. Many adults reminisce that learning how they best learn is the single most important thing they learned in school, because it unlocked the rest of their literate lives.

RESEARCH ABOUT THINKING ABOUT THINKING

The word *metacognition* first appeared in 1979 in the work of John Flavell from Stanford University, but the idea of teaching writing, reading, and thinking strategies to children has existed in education since John Dewey first theorized on reflection and inquiry in the early part of the twentieth century.

Although the research suggests that adults benefit from metacognitive strategies that they were neither explicitly taught or aware of using, 28 years of research has found that explicit instruction in metacognition in school-age children has measurable and long-term effects compared to comparison control groups, according to Emily Lai's literature review of metacognition research. Accepted as a word in the mid-1990s, metacognition celebrates its 20 years in the public eye with increased acceptance and knowledge, especially in education.

Research into neuroplasticity, the ability of even adult brains to change and heal after life change or injury, shows that changes in thinking can change the structure of the brain. Researchers like Donna Wilson and Marcus Conyers have found that explicitly teaching metacognitive strategies and about neuroplasticity to children dramatically improves academic performance and reorganizes brain functioning, knowing how to drive their brain makes a huge impact on their learning.

When learners apply their new knowledge in new ways or reflect on their learning, the newly laid neural pathways are strengthened and connected to established knowledge and learning patterns already existing in the brain. The newly learned material is thus easier to retrieve and lasts longer than material learned without the benefits of metacognition.

Many high school teachers are tempted to see a final writing as the end of that learning, yet reflection on the reading and writing process is needed to cement the acquisition of new skills. Department of Education analysis of California State University's Expository Reading and Writing Course shows that the reflection part of the modules are the least likely to be done by teachers but, when done, seem to increase the long-term benefit of the curriculum.

Most metacognition falls into three categories: task-oriented, cognitive functioning, and social emotional metacognition. The primary tasks in literacy classrooms, reading and writing, can only gain mastery by adding metacognitive strategies. The business of reading and writing is the collection of gaining metacognitive strategies.

While inquiry into scientific and mathematical processes may be less used in literacy classrooms, the metacognitive tasks of self-monitoring cognition and finding the best working patterns for their own brains is still the science of learning. As communication, written and spoken, is the work of our classrooms, the social emotional work of connecting to an audience requires metacognition and personal growth.

READING AND WRITING METACOGNITION

According to Barbara Sitko, the research into the metacognition involved with reading and writing shows that even though adults may not be aware of learning or using metacognitive strategies, it's not possible to reach higher levels of reading and writing without metacognition.

Excellent readers and writers do a long list of metacognitive strategies like checking for understanding, putting the ideas into different words, considering audience or author, etc., repeatedly. Being a good reader and writer goes beyond recall of facts or knowledge of procedures; experienced readers and writers use a variety of metacognitive strategies depending on the task.

GENERAL FUNCTIONING

Our conversations, our teacher talk, with students can help them learn the best way to drive their own cognitive functioning. Drs. Donna Wilson and Marcus Conyers, in their articles for the Association for Supervision and Curriculum Development (ASCD) and Edutopia, describe how any lesson can become metacognitive when teachers highlight *how* students are learning, not just *what* they are learning. Creating learning plans, managing stress and sleep plans, and experimenting on themselves to find their best learning patterns can be part of any classroom.

SOCIAL EMOTIONAL METACOGNITION

Social emotional metacognition involves learning how best to work, collaborate, and communicate with others. All humans have different social and emotional needs and strengths; learning that not everyone thinks and feels like you is an important part of maturing. Schools that make social emotional learning and metacognition part of the curriculum see happier, better adjusted, and higher performing academically students, according to Dr. Maurice Elias and others studying the effects of social and emotional learning on students.

Teaching Self-reflection

Learning without reflection is like framing a house without adding siding; reflection is what gives learning shape and protects it from degrading. Teachers can accomplish reflection of the day or the unit's learning with exit slips explaining what they learned that day, final conferences to reflect on learning, letters to reflect on learning, or even a pair-share of the day's learning, but no matter how reflection occurs, it appears that unexamined learning is quicker to degrade.

According to Henry Roediger III and Mark A. McDaniel in their book *Make It Stick*, explaining recent advances in learning theory, reflection increases the ability of a learner to lay-down the day's learning in long-term memory and increases recall and ability to apply learning to new settings. Research from the Harvard Business School on businesses suggests that experiences *only* become learning with reflection.

California State University Monterey Bay's University Writing Program coordinator Nelson Graff has written about transfer and college literacy. In the idea of transfer, researchers examine what literacy skills learned in literacy and language arts classrooms cross-over to other disciplines and settings.

No matter how successful students are in class, if they can't transfer those skills to voter pamphlets, workplace documents, or writing an email to their county to protect their home, our classes haven't been successful.

Using a variety of texts, teaching critical thinking, and reflection on learning are the key components to ensure that what happens in the classroom transfers to students' lives. While Common Core emphasizes different genres of text and critical thinking skills, consistent and regular opportunities to reflect on learning is the other necessary, and missing, ingredient for transfer of learning.

RETHINKING FEEDBACK TO MAKE STUDENTS EXPERTS ON THEIR OWN LEARNING

Literacy teachers give feedback. Written on papers, verbal in conferences and helping them in class, and nonverbal with our facial expressions and gestures: Students look, too much, to the judgment of their instructors. We want them to realize reading, writing, and speaking are about communicating, but students' intent on a grade, or approval, can miss the chance to be experts on their learning. Students are headed to a world where they will have to navigate communication without our judgment or the surety of a grade earned.

Teachers have so much content and skills to teach that it can be easy to forget that they must also teach students to trust their own judgment, be metacognitive. A simple switch is to ask students what they think, and then pause long enough for them to actually think it through, before providing them an answer. Literacy instructors tend to be expert readers and writers and can forget the time it takes to actually understand new metacognitive strategies, like annotation or reordering an argument. Struggle takes time, a scarce resource in classrooms, but struggle is where learning happens.

Some examples of ways to give feedback that promotes metacognition:

- What strategies could you use to understand the reading better?
- Where do you think you got stuck?
- I understand that you don't like your first paragraph. What do you think you could do to make it better?
- What make the model text appealing to read? How could you do that in your text?
- I agree that your conclusion could be better. How will you experiment to improve it?

Ideally, teacher feedback should give students more ownership of their reading and writing growth, acknowledging that learning unearthed is more valuable and long-lasting than ideas given.

METACOGNITIVE WRITING STRATEGIES

Have you ever heard that someone "writes like they talk?" Well, it's definitely true that we write like we think! Writing, to an audience or reflectively, is thinking on paper. As Barbara M. Sitko finds in her chapter "Knowing how to write: Metacognition and writing instruction" in the 1998 book *Metacognition in Educational Theory and Practice,* young children write in a free association way, listing or narrating everything they know about a topic, while older children are able to use more metacognitive strategies to consider audience needs, purpose of writing, and genre considerations.

Experienced writers also have more revision strategies and recursively move between the steps of planning, translating, and reviewing to constantly be reading their work, checking it against their goal in their mind, and then translating and reforming the texts used. Sitko reinforces the idea that reading and writing appear to use many of the same metacognitive strategies, and that the best writers have many tools in their toolbox to improve their writing.

Strategies for Emerging Writers

Sound out words	Question self: What else do I know?
Transition words	Dictation
Read aloud to understand	Draw pictures to aid understanding
Paragraph hamburger	Replacing unknown words with rebus

Strategies for Novice Writers

Edit mechanics	Peer editing
Descriptive writing	Reorder for clarity
Pair-share	Color coding claims, evidence, and analysis for revision
Writing conferences	
Read aloud to revise	

Strategies for Experienced Writers

Imagine an audience	Peer review
Writers workshop	Reorder for readability
Edit for genre	Rhetorically analyze own work

METACOGNITIVE READING STRATEGIES

This is a nonfiction book that tries to explain the implications of a branch of science, positive psychology, to an audience of literacy educators. Chapters introduce a topic from that science, explain the research, and connect to classroom practice. By the last chapter, none of this is news to you, an expert reader. Even if you weren't conscious of it, you used metacognitive reading strategies that you have accrued from decades of experience reading.

Remember, as referenced in the chapter on mastery, adults build and strengthen reading skills throughout their lives, despite the assumption that readers are done growing at high school graduation. Part of that assumption comes from the common practice of not explicitly teaching reading strategies after the elementary grades.

As children first learn to read, elementary teachers do an excellent job of guiding them to those introductory strategies: sound out the word, reread, read aloud, look at the words around it for help, and so on. Middle school teachers focus on sustaining the love of reading: high-interest choices, comfy places to lounge while reading, protected reading times, book clubs, and reading prizes. It seems though that somewhere along the way reading strategies gets deemphasized, until students are no longer conscious that they are gaining reading strategies.

Elementary programs like Reading Rockets and middle and high school programs like Reading Apprenticeship from WestEd explicitly teach reading instruction through grade 16. Reading Rockets, a federally funded website and community of literacy instructors and researchers, has blogs and strategies for elementary and middle school students.

Strategies for Emerging Readers

Sound out words	Check pictures to confirm reading
Read with a friend	Story sequence
Read aloud	Follow words with finger
Word wall	Think-Pair-Share

Strategies for Novice Readers

Survey the text	Stop and paraphrase
Context clues for vocabulary	List-Group-Label
Reciprocal teaching	Summarizing
Personal response to text in margin	Anticipation guide

Strategies for Experienced Readers

Annotation	Question the author
Rhetorical analysis	Highlight claims and evidence in different colors
Write "a conversation" between sources	Consider effectiveness of order
Concept map	
Descriptive outlining	

METACOGNITIVE COLLABORATION STRATEGIES

Is this working? What are our strengths? Learning to check in emotionally and socially with collaborators is a necessary metacognitive skill. Teacher talk that models treating students as valued contributors, acknowledges needing different interpersonal strengths in effective groups, and holds students accountable for their ability to work with others can positively influence student collaboration. Some teachers describe this shift as moving from authoritarian to coach, highlighting the idea of empowering students to drive their own learning.

Literature circles with roles, writer's chair, and reading jigsaws are all examples of teaching practices intended to teach collaboration, but reflection on interpersonal strengths is the required metacognitive practice to make those experiences into learning about working with others.

Before, during, and after collaborative learning, students should be asked to reflect on their strengths in working with a group and to anticipate problems and how they will deal with them, best practices for dealing with different personalities, preferred communication methods for their group, and expected contributions of each group member. Corporations continue to tell educators that effective collaboration, not dysfunctional group work, needs to be taught more in schools.

MODELING METACOGNITIVE STRATEGIES

Teacher preparation courses and professional organizations have been promoting reflective teaching for at least the last twenty-five years. The idea reinforces the philosophy that teachers are professionals who must reflect on their practice to improve—in short, be metacognitive. Teaching requires all of the forms of metacognition: task, cognitive, and social emotional. Many teachers have made daily, weekly, monthly, and/or yearly reflections part of their practice, to the benefit of themselves and their students. Edutopia has a wealth of knowledge about teacher metacognitive practices if you would like to learn more about educator reflections.

A missed opportunity, then, is not pulling back the curtain a bit for that practice and modeling metacognition more to students. Thinking aloud to pull apart a reading or writing task demonstrates to students that even experts are just stringing together strategies. Modeling goal setting and cognitive metacognition helps students think about their own thinking process after getting a peek at their instructor's.

Deliberate transparency describing interpersonal processes, like sharing that a need for visuals encourages some to keep notes in group meetings, helps them think through their own interpersonal strengths. Asking for student feedback on teaching may make you feel vulnerable, but it transmits the value that everyone, even the teacher, is learning and growing here.

TEACHERS AND WRITERS TALK

I love metacognition! That was the huge epiphany of teaching when I finally realized that the most valuable thing I can and do teach is the ability to think about how you think. For example, a recent conversation with a student went like this:

> *Student: This is the worst score I've ever had.*
>
> *Me: Well, okay, I'm not going to argue it wasn't.*
>
> *We were about to sit down and use reflection and metacognition, but she beat me to it.*
>
> *Student: Normally, I do really well because I do this. I didn't this time because I did this. Next time, I can do this.*

Metacognition is the game-changer that allows them to be in charge and not need teachers to pass down judgment, but to be the coach that listens to their self-analysis and helps them to find strategies to be their best.

—Gini Wozny

About Gini: Gini Wozny teaches in an early college high school, Academy of the Redwoods, and mentors new teachers.

Take-away: Teaching metacognitive strategies ultimately empowers students to continue their learning with less and less teacher input, preparing them for a life outside of school.

> *One of the best ways teachers can model metacognition is through the inquiry process. As a social studies teacher who has been involved on the advocacy front in my state, I've worked with other educators in the revision of our state Social Studies frameworks. The foundation for these frameworks is inquiry, a process by which students, with the guidance and support of the teacher, develop compelling and supporting questions that will guide their learning. In a sense, all true learning is inquiry, and the most meaningful and enduring learning is that which is significant and relevant to students, to their interests, and to their understanding of the world around them. When engaged in inquiry, students are continuously thinking and reflecting on the learning process, what questions need to be asked, and what steps need to be taken. Furthermore, in order to actively and meaningfully engage in such learning, they must be prepared and have the skills to critically analyze the process, their sources, their findings, and*

their product. Such learning is intrinsically motivated and contributes to the development of autonomy, agency, efficacy, and growth.

—David Bosso

About David: Researcher, champion of teacher leadership, former Connecticut Teacher of the Year, and academic David Bosso surveyed teachers on best practices, their inspiration, and the ways they were intrinsically motivated. Bosso advocates for teacher and student reflection toward growth.

Take-away: Like many researchers, Bosso has concluded that learning without metacognitive inquiry is shallow and aimed at recall, not understanding. Like many teachers, Bosso has also found that learning without reflection has little staying power.

On every standardized English test we give ELLs, we ask them to "choose one and give two reasons why." That has been my springboard for coaching my students toward metacognition. At the end of an activity, I ask my students was this assignment easy or challenging for you? If they choose one, then give two reasons why it was easy or challenging, I see them identifying their own strengths (as in, "This was easy for me because it's the third time we have practiced this") and labeling their ongoing challenges. In the latter, I find a troubling quantity of fixed mindset statements. (As in, "I'm not good at writing.") Though these statements are troubling, asking students to generate these responses allows for a frank discussion of the power of language and self-talk. After this, subsequent responses tend to lean toward the "yet" statements. ("I'm not good at writing yet.") Just that shift allows us to frame the rest of the year's discussion of learning in growth mindset terms and positive self-talk. As their skills develop, I can ask broader questions with more specific responses. For instance, I introduced the continuum to them two months ago. Now I ask them to rate their opinions on a continuum and then explain, as well as rate their confidence and competence with skills we are practicing. Their responses are becoming more nuanced as the year progresses.

—Raven Coit

About Raven: Experienced English language development teacher Raven Coit uses reflection and metacognition with students who are English language learners.

Take-away: Metacognition and its impact on neuroplasticity allow for faster and more effective academic growth than the same instruction without teacher talk aimed at growing metacognition.

Smith and Wilhelm, in Going with the Flow, *describe showing students the road and the path for engaging in their work in reading and writing. They base their approach largely on George Hillocks's research that suggests the best approach to teaching writing is to establish group problem-solving activities that engage* students in surfacing their tacit knowledge about the procedures needed to generate content for their writing. Smith and Wilhelm apply a similar approach to literature instruction. That approach, combined with WestEd's Reading Apprenticeship—which involves attending to four dimensions of the learning experience—personal, social, cognitive, and knowledge-building and centers around metacognitive conversation—help to foster mastery and transfer.

I'm a big fan of a few key strategies. 1) Small-group problem-solving activities. In small groups, students are often highly engaged because of their social interaction. If the problems are themselves engaging and encourage disagreement, students end up discussing their strategies for solving problems in the process of coming to agreement (or considered disagreement). 2) I like to begin class by asking students what was challenging about their work the night before and how they engaged with those challenges. If we begin by valuing struggle, we help students learn strategies from each other and learn that difficulty is a place to start, not to end. 3) I like to model by using think-alouds and then have students do think-alouds with each other.

—*Nelson Graff*

About Nelson: Nelson Graff, University Writing Program director at California State University Monterey Bay, writes and researches about curriculum and transfer.

Take-away: Metacognitive strategies, for both reading and writing, foster mastery and transfer.

LEARN MORE

What to Read

- FitzGerald, William T. "The Problem of Transfer, or What Students Misplace Along the Way." *TMAC/New Faculty Connections Workshop. Rutgers–Camden, NJ: TMAC*, 2013.

  The notes from this talk take on the history of transfer research, writing tasks that promote transfer, and research on how reflection cements learning.

- Graff, Nelson. "Teaching Rhetorical Analysis to Promote Transfer of Learning." *Journal of Adolescent & Adult Literacy* 53.5 (2010): 376–85. Web.

  Graff's work discussing the metacognitive strategies necessary for mastery and transfer help college and university instructors prepare students, not only for their composition classes but also for other college classes and their careers.

- "Instruction of Metacognitive Strategies Enhances Reading Comprehension and Vocabulary Achievement of Third-Grade Students." *Reading Rockets*. WETA Public Broadcasting, Web.

This website and program, funded by the U.S. Department of Education, is a resource for strategies, reading blogs, and reading strategy videos for parents, educators, and librarians.

- Lai, Emily R. "Metacognition: A Literature Review." *Pearson Assessments*, 2011. Web. http://images.pearsonassessments.com/images/tmrs/metacognition_literature_review_final.pdf.

  This forty-one-page literature review of metacognitive research history has some compelling conclusions about the effect of explicit instruction in metacognition and cooperative learning.

- Top 20 Principles from Psychology for PreK–12 Teaching and Learning. APA Report. Washington, DC: American Psychological Association, 2015. Web.

  Principle 7 of this report on bringing psychological research to the classroom argues that self-regulation and reflection can and should be taught for students to take charge of their learning.

- "Research & Impact." *Reading Apprenticeship at WestEd*. San Francisco, CA: WestEd, 2016. Web.

  Reading Apprenticeship is a metacognitive reading program aimed at middle school, high school, and college instructors and students.

- Sitko, Barbara M. "Knowing How to Write: Metacognition and Writing Instruction." *Metacognition in Educational Theory and Practice*. Mahwah, NJ: Erlbaum, 1998. 93–116. Web.

  Sitko's analysis of the research on metacognitive writing reviews work from the Center for the Study of Writing and Literacy and the National Writing Project, among others, and categorizes the stages of metacognition in the writing process.

- Wilson, Donna, and Marcus Conyers. "The Boss of My Brain." *Educational Leadership: Instruction That Sticks*. ASCD 72.2 (Oct. 2014). Web. Sept. 5, 2016.

  Researchers Wilson and Conyers argue for more metacognition instruction in schools in their books and online articles.

What to Watch

- "Good Thinking! That's So Meta(cognitive)!" YouTube. Smithsonian Science Education Center, Nov. 10, 2015. Web.

  This animated video explains how to integrate metacognitive strategies into lessons about other subjects. Teacher talk prompting metacognitive thinking can make any subject expand students' thinking about thinking.

Conclusion

So, if you've read all the way to the end, you've discovered that the last forty years of research on intrinsic motivation have explored why we do what we do, and what we do in education can be done better. It's time to do better.

We've learned about growth mindset, rewards, autonomy, mastery, purpose, connection, recognition, and metacognition. It may seem like too much to juggle in your teacher brain along with the curriculum and all of your students' names. So, just for you, for slogging through all of that research, here are five distilled ideas.

1. **Give Them Curriculum That Matters**
   If you, as the adult in the room, who's the expert on the topic, don't know why you're teaching a particular skill, reading, or worksheet, skip it. Skip it. Our time with them is too short and too precious to teach them a curriculum that doesn't pique their interest, excite them, anger them, give them a new way of seeing themselves, or offer new life choices.

   Curriculum can connect to service learning, learning about their communities or families, global citizenship, the environment they will breathe for the next sixty years, or their varied and ever-changing interests. Often the best curriculum connects them to each other at the same time, as it makes them see people thousands of miles away as people just like them.

   In language arts, we also have a chance for them to connect their reading and writing inwards. We are all on a passage of self-discovery, but childhood has the newest waters and adolescence the most turbulence; it's fascinating stuff. Writing is a chance to find out what you think; ask them to write to communicate to you and their congressional representative, but also to learn the workings of their own brain.

As literacy arts teachers, there is no denying that we have a distinct advantage here. What can matter more than who we are, how we communicate and connect to others, what it means to be human, and what will their futures look like?

2. Let Them Make More Choices

Trust them to want to read, write, think, and speak, by giving them more choices in the classroom. If teachers want students to act intrinsically motivated, teachers must trust students with more choices. Students make educational choices, whether you allow it or not, by choosing to do the homework or care or engage. When students can choose their readings, their stance on a topic, the order they write the paper, or how best to revise, they begin to own their learning, engaging in the process. It belonged to them all along.

Teachers want students to be successful after they leave their current classroom. Student success comes with giving them steadily more choices as they show that they can handle them. Just as first graders may not be able to handle choosing their seat mate without guidance, sophomores may need teachers to choose their blogging privacy settings until they show they can handle it. Giving up control to students this way is one of the purposes of education.

3. What Matters Hurts, So Be with Them Through the Hurt

When students and staff risk by showing what matters to them, they will feel exposed. Our classrooms and schools need to be safe places to be exposed, safe places to show who we are. There are few scarier activities than showing others your writing or public speaking, because, in both cases, you show who you are. Classrooms must be emotionally safe before that can happen well.

Having curriculum that matters and making choices is a recipe for hurt. If students write blog pals in Morocco or debate current issues in class, they will sometimes get their hearts broken or feelings hurt. If they dare to enter a writing contest, they may not win. The emotional connection that students feel to their teacher and classmates will affect their academic success.

4. Really Allow the Writing Process and Its Mess

Writing is messy. It can be tempting to put it in a lock-step process that can be put on a time-table and formed into regularly scheduled assessments. Except writers tell us that it's a process. It goes in circles between composition and revision, it comes in fits and starts, and some parts of the process take different amounts of time for different people.

As the complexity of the thinking and writing tasks increases with the years in school, so will the mess. That mess doesn't fit necessarily with progress reports, and five classes a day, and all of the practicalities of school.

Teachers will have to explore ways to allow for that mess and creation, portfolios or blogs or flexible deadlines or whatever experiment helps.

Also, teaching is messy. Like writing, it's hard to do well at first, there will be revisions, and there will be days that it's easier than others. Be just as patient and compassionate with yourself those days as you are with those new writers; everyone will find their way.

5. Celebrate Their Humanity

The human brain amazes scientists still with its ability to learn, imagine, create, love, and change. Teachers do not teach facts and minutiae; we teach nothing less than how to grow minds. Students grow in abilities in our classrooms, but they also grow in knowledge of selves, personal drive, ownership of their futures, and self-reliance. Growing together is enough reason to celebrate our journey together into our humanity.

Index

agency. *See* autonomy
Allison, Maria, 32
Amabile, Teresa, 17, 20, *22*
American Psychological Association (APA), *24*, 80
Armstrong, Thomas, 51, 55
attendance, ix, 16, 19, 23
Atwell, Nancie, 52
audiences, 5, 11, 60, 65–67
autonomous support, 23
autonomy, 17, 22, 26, 27, 47–56, 62, 67, 71, 77, 82. *See also* choice(s)

backward planning, 60, 61
behavior modification, 20
Berninger, Virginia, 6
Bettinger, Eric, 19
Blackwell, Lisa, 2
blogs, 11, 56, 66–67, 68, 70, 71. *See also* digital publishing
Bosso, David, 27, 42, 71, 96–97
"broaden and build," 33, 75–76
Burgess, David, 69

Caruso, H. M., 80
Change the World (program), 63
checklist grading, 51, 54
Chen, Huan, 77
Chenot, David, 10

choice(s), 48–49, 54–56; controlling, *48*; effects of, 50; format and, 49, 51–52; mobility and, 49, 52–53; pace and, 49, 50–51, 55; reading, *48*, 50, *53*, 102; supportive, *48*; topic and, 48, 49, 52, 102; writing, *52*. *See also* autonomy
Churchill, Winston, 33
classroom management, 42
cognitive growth, 17, 19, 20, 79
Coit, Raven, vii–viii, 49, 78, 84–85, 97
collaboration, 71, 79, 80, 81, 83, 85, 91, 95
Common Core, 7, 32, 39, *48*, 50, 60, 65, 80, 92
community service, 21, 62–63
competence, 9, 13, 17, 19, *24*, 32–33, 34, 35, *36*, 40, 41, 47, 50, 59, 71, 77, 78, 97
competition, 20, 27
compliance, ix, 27
conferences, 5, 25, 35, 41, 65, 91, 92; digital writing, 67; letters, 38
connection, 17, 20, 25, 26, 75–86. *See also* relatedness
content, 42, 51, 92
control, x, 26, 47; and choices, *48*; controlling factor, 22; controlling language, *24*, 25, 49; wanting, 54. *See also* locus of control

Index

Conyers, Marcus, 90, 91
cooperative learning, 80, *81*, 85–86
creativity, 17, 19, 20, 27–28, 75
Csikszentmihalyi, Mihaly, x, 15, 32, 59
culture: classroom, 39, 75, 78, 79, 84, 102; school, 19, 21, 33, 38, 61, 75, 78–79, 83–84, 102

Deci, Edward, ix, x, 15, 17, 18, *22*, *24*, 25, 26, 32, *48*, 49, 50, 54, 59
Dewey, John, 89
digital publishing, 11, 39, 66, 70
document sharing, 67
Downing, Melanie, 10, 56
Duncan, Margaret Carlisle, 32
Dweck, Carol, x, 1–2, 8, 10, *22*, *24*, 71

effort, 2, 7, 9, 19, 23, 33, *77*
Elias, Maurice J., 55, 63, 69–70, 79, 91
engagement, ix, x, 49, 50, 59, 62, 67, 69
English Language Learners (ELLs), 39, 97
Epley, Nicholas, 15
eudaimonism, 76
Expository Reading and Writing Curriculum (ERWC), 39, 40, 61, 90

failure, 2, 3, *8*, 12, 34, 38, 83
feedback, 1–2, 5, 8–9, 10, 25, 26, 56, 76, 82, 92, 96
Flavell, John, 89
flow, 32, 42, 59
formative assessment, 35
food insecurity, 20
Francia, Rose Sita, 20
Fredrickson, Barbara, x, 33, 75

gamification, 47–56
Gehringer, Carrie Ann, 70
genius hour, 59, 60, 61
Gifted and Talented Education (GATE), 35
global education, 70–71, 101

goal(s): profit/purpose, 59; setting, 2, 11, 32, 34–35, *36–37*, 39, 41, 49, 64, 80, 95
grades, 16, 22, 34, 51, 59, 64
Graff, Nelson, 53, 91, 97–98
Grant, Adam, 59

Halstead, Pam, 85
happiness, 80, 91
high-stakes testing, 22, 34
Hill, Graham, 10
Hillocks, George, 97–98
Howell, Colleen J., 10
Howell, Ryan T., 10
Huebner, E. Scott, 77

incentives, 16, 19–20
inquiry learning, 60, 61, 79, *81*, 85, 89, 96
inverse grading, 51, 54

Jager, Lisa, 11–12, 41
Jordan, Michael, 5

Kajtaniak, Tara Nuth, 70–71
Kappes, Heather Barry, 9
Katz, Mira-Lisa, 40
King, Stephen, 31
Kohn, Alfie, 76, 85

Lai, Emily, 89
learned helplessness, 48, 54
learning, 20, *22*, 25, 27, 31, 38, 49, 59, 75, 76, 85, 90, 96; goals, 32–33, 41, 42, 60, 67, 68; presentation of, 51, 55; types, *81*
Locke, Edwin, 33
locus of control: external, 23, 48; internal, 47–48

Malone, Thomas, 49
mastery, viii, 9, 25, 26, 31–43, 55, 60, 67, 76, 90, 98
Mather, Nancy, 35–36
Mayerson, Neal, 82

McDaniel, Mark A., 3, 9, 31, 91
Mendling, Barbara K., 35–36
metacognition, 3, 19, 21, *37*, 38, 69, 89–98; and cognitive functioning, 90, 91, 95; social emotional, 90, 91–92, 95; task-oriented, 90, 92, 95
mindset: fixed, 2, 4, *8*, 12, 35, 97; growth, vii–viii, 1–12, 22, 35, 55, 70, 71, 97, 101
Mitchell, Richard, 32
Mondrian, Piet, 31
motivation, *48*, 62, 71, 77; extrinsic, viii, 17–18, 25, 27, 76; intrinsic, viii, ix, x, 16, 18, 19, 22, 25, 26, 27, 32, 33, 42, 49, 50, 59, 60, 69, 70, 75, 101, 102; self-limiting, 17; teacher, 16, 26–27
multiple intelligences, 51–52, 55
Muraven, Mark, 77

National Council of Teachers of English, 15, 39
National Writing Project, 15, 35, 39, 82
neuroplasticity, 89–90, 97
Niemiec, Christopher, 59

Partnership for 21st Century Learning, 79, 80
peer review, 39, 82, *93*
performance, 5, 9, 15–16, 19, 22–23, 26, 64–65, 90
perseverance, 2, 33, 53, 75, 77
Peterson, Chris, 82
Pink, Daniel, ix, *8*, 11, 26–27
portfolios, 5, 25, 34–35, 38, 39, 51, 54, 66, 67, 102
positive peer pressure, 19
positive psychology, ix–x, 1, 69, 75–76, 82, 93
positivity, 75–86
praise, *8*, *24*, 25, 76, *77*
Praise, Question, Wish, 82
process-oriented guided inquiry learning (POGIL), 79, 81, 85

professional development, 15, 40–41, 62, 71
project-based learning (PBL), 16, 59, 60, 61, 79, 81
purpose, 16, 26, 39, 41, 50, 59–71, 76, 78. *See also* relevance

read-aloud, 81
Reading Apprenticeship, 94
Reading Rockets, 94
recognition, 15–27, 83
Reder, Stephen, 40
reflection, 10, 12, 42, 71, 89, 90, 91–92, 93, 95, 96, 97
Reid, Alex, 10
relatedness, 17, 71, 77–78. *See also* connection
relevance, *37*, 59–71, 77; reading, *68*; speaking, *65*; writing, *67*. *See also* purpose
restitution programs, 21
revision, 2, 34, 50, 55, 82, 102
rewards, 15–27, 77–78; extrinsic, 19, *22*, 27, 76
Roberts, Rhia, 35–36
Roediger, Henry L., 3, 9, 31, 91
Rogers, Carl, 77
Rotter, Julian, 47, 48
Rowling, J. K., 47
Ryan, Richard, ix, x, 15, 17, 18, *22*, *24*, 25, 32, 49, 54, 59

Sanborn, Alex, 54–55
self-assessment, 39
self-determination theory, ix, 16, 17, 18, 32, 48, 71, 77
Seligman, Martin, x, 33, 48, 54, 82
service learning, 59, 62–63, 69, 70, 79, 101
shame, 22, 64
silent reading, 21
Sitko, Barbara, 90, 93
Smith, Michael, 97–98
social and emotional learning (SEL), 63, 79, 85, 91

special education, 35, 38–39
standardized testing, 22–23, 25
strategies: metacognitive, 89–98; reading, 40, 89, *94*; revision, 93; speaking, 65; writing, 40, 89, *93*
strength-based character education, 19, 33, 82–84
supportive language, *25*

Tate, Ryan, 16, 61
Tian, Lili, 77
transfer, 91–92, 98
transparency, 41–42, 60, 95
Trout, Laura, 81

VIA Institute, 82
volunteerism, 48, 63

Weiner, Bernard, 47
Wigfield, Allan, 57
Wilhelm, Jeffrey, 97–98
Williams, Jasmine D., 49
willpower, 77. *See also* perseverance
Wilson, Donna, 90, 91
Wooley, A. W., 80
Wozny, Gini, 41–42, 55–56, 96
writer's chair, 39, 65, 81, 95
writers' workshop, 39, 79, 82, 93
writing process, 39, 50, 57, 102; endurance in, 5, 6; flexibility in, 5; speed in, 5, 6–7; strength in, 5, 6; technique in, 5, 7

Yolen, Jane, 4

About the Author

Amy K. Conley, trained in working with at-risk learners and teaching adult literacy with a degree in psychology and journalism, currently teaches English 12 Expository Reading and Writing Curriculum, English 9, and academic writing for other teachers. She also writes curriculum for the California State University's Expository Reading and Writing Curriculum for middle school and researches and writes about positive psychology in education.

She is a happy resident of Fortuna, California, along with her two kids, partner, and cats.

www.ingramcontent.com/pod-product-compliance
Lightning Source LLC
Chambersburg PA
CBHW030145240426
43672CB00005B/284